THE ALMOST DANCER

JESSICA RIBERA

White Blackbird
BOOKS

ISBN-13:978-1-7340181-2-7

Cover design by Blaze Bratcher

Photo by Elisabeth Haggard

ALSO BY WHITE BLACKBIRD BOOKS

All Are Welcome: Toward a Multi-Everything Church

Birth of Joy: Philippians

Choosing a Church: A Biblical and Practical Guide

Ever Light and Dark: Telling Secrets, Telling the Truth

Everything Is Meaningless? Ecclesiastes

FirstFruits of a New Creation: Essays Honoring Jerram Barrs

Heal Us, Emmanuel: A Call for Racial Reconciliation, Representation, and Unity in the Church

The Organized Pastor: Systems to Care for People Well

A Sometimes Stumbling Life: Making Sense of Our Struggles and God's Grace in the Journey of Faith

Urban Hinterlands: Planting the Gospel in Uncool Places

Follow whiteblackbirdbooks.pub for upcoming titles and releases.

PRAISE FOR THE ALMOST DANCER

More than a tale of loss, *The Almost Dancer* is simultaneously a tender coming-of-age story set in the rarified world of elite ballet training and a nuanced, hopeful look at the power of nurturing dreams into adulthood. Jessica Ribera deftly balances grief and grace in her compelling memoir; with a sharp eye for detail and overflowing hunger for life, she poignantly recounts the journey from dance student, to almost dancer, to dancer once more. Her love for ballet is palpable on every page, and her earnest reflections on faith, pain, and meaning resonate long after the final chapter.

Laurel Simon
Dancer, Instructor, Choreographer

Life *is* a dance. But not the one we expect. Jessica gracefully guides us to this truth through her own unexpected journey, and we are blessed to have such a good instructor.

Scott Erickson
Visual Artist and Author

The Almost Dancer transcends the world of ballet, capturing the tragic and trivial moments that define any adolescence. Jessica tells us what it feels like to be a young woman on the brink of achieving her dream. Simple, honest, and moving, this book is also rare—we don't usually get to hear the testimonies of the nearly successful.

Carla Wright
Former Professional Dancer

Jessica Ribera's captivating transparency and spiritual depth make her a wonderful guide for anyone experiencing loss or wrestling through their own vocations.

Amy Peterson
Author of *Where Goodness Still Grows* and *Dangerous Territory*

This book is terribly important, and I am so grateful to have read it. It is for aspiring dancers, for former dancers, for jaded dancers, for non-dancers. It contains both searing loss and brilliant hope, clad in honesty and poetry, laughter and tears. But above all, the exploration of Jessica's developing theology of suffering is critical for all of us here 'in the middle' - waiting for the culmination of all things, for what is to come but is not yet. It is this truth that I hope her readers do not miss.

Brittanie Wooten
Director, Doxa Dance

The Almost Dancer is a witty, existentially honest, and artistically written memoir-like piece. Ribera beautifully chronicles her *dream-pursued-to-dream-permanently-paused* journey. And by the way, there are great lessons for the church in this piece; namely, it is best to give those who are disappointed about a *dream-permanently-paused* the ministry of listening and presence and not an explanation. This book will not disappoint.

Luke Bobo
Visiting Professor in Contemporary Culture, Covenant Theological Seminary

The Almost Dancer shows us through its own graceful storytelling that the good life cannot simply be about following your dreams and ambition. For everyone who thought life might turn out one way and then it went sideways, *The Almost Dancer* shows us a richer story of faith, renewal, and how there is a gift wrapped up in our fears, failures, and losses.

Ashley Hales
Author of *Finding Holy in the Suburbs*

This book is easy to read, not clunky, or pretentious. It left a tender and hopeful mark without any wrapping-up-in-a-bow feeling.
Elizabeth Miller Hayes
Author of *Ever Light and Dark*

It's true: This book is for anyone who loves ballet, from the stage or audience. But after we walk behind the curtain of the dance world, we walk deeper into the story of a woman living one life but ultimately loving another, and finding her full self along the way. This book is for the dreamers, the broken down, the faithful, the doubting, the faith-filled, and the overcoming ones. Which is a long way of saying this story is for all of us.
Sara Billups
Faith and Culture Writer

For anyone who has suffered loss, the crushing weight of losing who you are and no longer knowing which way to go, this story will speak to you. Ribera delves into disintegrating pain and in so doing finds herself, recovers her identity, and reclaims her losses. Nothing will take away the tragedy in her life, but for this dancer the story doesn't end there.
Karen Morton, M.A., LMHC
Individual, Couple, & Adolescent Therapist

A remarkably raw and unfiltered glimpse at life behind the shiny curtain. Heartfelt, tragic, bittersweet, and triumphant, *The Almost Dancer* has all the elements of a gripping classical ballet, and proves that while all that glitters may not be gold, every cloud has a silver lining.
Laura Tisserand
Principal Dancer, Pacific Northwest Ballet

Like a real-life Noel Streatfeild heroine all grown up, Jessica Ribera wrestles with the drive to dance, the narrow and sometimes abusive world of professional ballet, and how to keep the gifts from the journey in her life while letting go of the destination. A charming, tender look at the passion and dedication of an exuberant young dancer, and the mourning process of losing a dream and embracing her family and God with a new sense of purpose in motherhood and as a budding writer.

Allison K. Williams
Social Media Editor, *Brevity Magazine*

The Almost Dancer is an emotionally moving memoir about a journey of training in the professional ballet world. Ribera writes about her hopes and dreams for a ballerina career from the very first day of her ballet training. Her colorful use of metaphors and attention to stimulating details give the reader an environment to become immersed in, to feel like you are sitting in the ballet studio at that very moment. Through Ribera's writing the reader is allowed to connect with her childhood dreams, journey through inspiring and devastating moments, and learn what it is like to pursue a passion from a place of vulnerability and grace. *The Almost Dancer* is a book that will inspire you to follow your dreams, cherish the struggle, and realize that there is always more to reach for.

Julie Tobiason
Principal Dancer (Pacific Northwest Ballet), Instructor, Director

CONTENTS

*This book is for young children
with big ideas doing hard work.*

PROGRAM NOTES

In the Amarillo neighborhood of my childhood, one section of houses had no alleyways but rather concealed a path through grass and young fruit trees. On walks with my family, we loved to see the crabapple-apple tree, a confusing but beautiful twist of two distinct types of tree that had grown together as one. Some branches bore white blossoms, while others produced the fluffy pink crabapple flowers. They could not have been separated.

Music and dance are the same for me, distinct but dependently oriented toward each other. With ballet training knitting the synapses of my brain from a young age, I sometimes feel like the third party in a braid of music and dance. The sound of music immediately translates into movement in my mind, often to the point of distraction. Decades of hyper-awareness to every tune in the air has led to popular music becoming a meaningful score. Any story I have worth telling has a song to go with it, so I have listed song titles to accompany nearly every chapter.

I trust the reader to engage with music however is convenient and feels best.

* * *

A word about protection: my rubric has been to write from my perspective alone while treating others as I want to be treated. Trouble is: I'm very open. My dad wonderfully said to me once, "Jessica, you put stuff on the internet that I don't even tell myself." Certainly true. Whether this quality is a blessing or a curse depends on your risk aversion.

This is, I admit, a young woman's writing. In the writing, I did not have the benefit of advanced age and perspective. So there are undoubtedly some jagged edges and imperfect conclusions. The only preventative measures I knew to take were to write scenes truthfully, never report others' motives or feelings, and call my guesses exactly that: guesses. Each real name that you see here represents respect, value, and, very often, a conversation resulting in permission. Hopefully I have chosen relationship over the cheap but tasty morsel of gossipy revelation.

When I grow up, I want to be a dancer.
If God does not want me to I won't be one.
I'll be whatever God wants me to be,
even a missionary.

Jessica Meador, age 7

PROLOGUE

Driving on the state highway, I pretended to hold a long, razor-sharp saw out my window. It could slice through fence posts, cows, telephone poles, trees, anything non-metal. I had to yank it back in quickly to keep from slicing metal lamp-posts, or the saw would crumple and pull me out the window to my bloody death on the pavement. I played this game every time I rode in the car.

I'm sure I'd been there as a baby and toddler, but the first time I remember driving to "the canyon," I played my game on the way and asked, "What does it look like?" *Canyon* was not in my regular vocabulary. "It looks like a hole in the ground," Dad said. I kept my eyes peeled as I felled the fences. A hole in the ground? I don't remember what I pictured, but I remember the reality.

The undulating grassy land populated with cattle and yucca suddenly dropped into a jagged, enormous, well, hole in the ground. I couldn't see it until we were right upon it. Rocky cliff walls faced one another closely, as if in private conversation, and formed a narrow chasm. I forgot all about my invisible saw. We crested a swell not big enough to call a hill, and there the whole beautiful canyon lay before us in reds and yellows. Here was a realm of endless possibility.

Walking into a dance studio for the first time produced that same sense of adventure.

* * *

To get ready for ballet class, I first had to decide to go. Emotions needed managing—excitement, fear, insecurity. Even joy must be controlled, because too much makes the dancing weird.

I choose pink tights, black for rebellious days. A safety pin gathers the neckline of my leotard right at the base of my sternum. The V shape elongates the neck and highlights the taught tendons of the throat. I pull sweatpants over the leotard and tights and top myself in a soft, wide-necked, hand-cut t-shirt that brags some workshop I attended.

Looking in the mirror (though I could do it with my eyes shut), I put a few bobby pins in my mouth and scrape my frizzy curls into a perfectly smooth ponytail. I divide the ponytail into two sections and begin rolling them in the same direction to form a cinnamon roll shape. Prying each pin slightly open with my teeth, I hook the edge of the twisting hair and plunge the pin back toward the inside beneath the hairband. I capture the stray hairs at the nape of my neck and at my temples with clips that flatten to the curve of my head and spray it all to kingdom come with Aqua Net.

I wrap a scarf around my waist and tuck it tightly to warm my lower back. The hole in the sole of my seamed tights stretches open to go over my foot and arrange just-so above my ankle bones. I put on my cardy-knit, fur-lined boots and scuff to the studio with my feet splayed out and my simple dance bag over my shoulder.

Inside, I find my place at the barre, flop the bag and then

my body to the floor. The thick rubber covering the floor is called "marley." First I lie on my belly with my legs in a diamond shape like a frog's. Inner thighs, knees, and ankle bones all touch the floor. I prop up on my elbows and chat with whoever isn't crabby. Soon, I swing my legs up into a spread-eagle split and raise my body up to sitting. If ribbons need sewing, I use white, waxed dental floss to attach them to my pointe shoes, being careful not to pierce the satin, only the canvas lining inside. My sewing kit has scissors, floss, ribbons, elastic, and a lighter which is used to melt the edge of the ribbon so that it will not fray. I cut the satin off the circular tip of the pointe shoe, and depending on who made the shoe, may use a giant bottle of superglue to reinforce the box and shank. The box is the part that encases the ball of my foot and toes. The shank is the stiff, inner sole. If that shank isn't cut down to only reach three-quarters of the way up the bottom of my foot, I do it myself.

I pull trifold paper towels that I have taken by the handful from bathroom dispensers out of my bag and fold exactly one paper towel around the toes of each foot before pulling my tights down over them to hold them in place. I slide on my pointe shoes, check for painful places, make adjustments to my paper towels, and add foam rubber Band-Aids where I need them. I have cut the ribbons to a perfect length for the knot to land on the inside of my ankle in the notch between my Achilles and the bone.

Now I stand. I face the barre and place my hands. I rock my feet back and forth from heel to ball to pointe. Deep *pliés* move me like an elevator. I swing my legs like a scythe each in turn either moving front to back or from side to side. Every stuck joint gets its turn for pops and clicks. I turn away from the barre and use my elbows to press the barre into my spine, cracking the vertebrae that need it. When the teacher opens the door, I take off my warm-ups, ball them into my bag, and toss it to the corner of the room. I finally take a moment to inventory what I'm hiding. Injuries, stress, conflicts with friends, trouble at home—all must be concealed.

OK, let's begin.

PART I

TINY DANCER

Ballerina, you must have seen her dancing in the sand
And now she's in me, always with me, tiny dancer in my hand

Elton John
"Tiny Dancer" from *Madman Across the Water*

A boyfriend had beat up his pregnant girlfriend again. This was usually why we went, though sometimes we were trying to get someone safe before a boyfriend came back. Pulling into the apartment lot, I settled to wait in the back seat while Mom walked up to a client's apartment. I always felt honored to be included in my mother's volunteer work for the Amarillo Area Crisis Pregnancy Center, but I felt afraid too. The smell of ash and cigarettes seeped into the car while I settled into waiting. A moment from the school gym came to mind.

While other first graders bounced dodge balls and crushed their fingers beneath the wheels of small rolling skateboards, I was transfixed by dust motes dancing in the light and thought:

Why am I here? What should I be doing? I mulled over the existential crisis for a long time in kid-years. Big questions kept popping up: *Why don't I like it here? Why do I worry all the time?* I couldn't put my finger on any specific answers, but I decided two things: 1) Staring and thinking are exercises that feel good and seem to be worth doing. 2) I wanted to leave Texas.

Mom finally came out of the building, dissipating the musings. "What happened?" I quickly asked.

"He kicked her in her stomach," Mom said. "Her stomach! And he knows she's pregnant!"

Later on, playing with Barbie, I tried to shake off the events of the day. I could only think about how Barbie's blonde hair looked just like the client's. Did Barbie get beat up? I generally wished I had a Ken, but right then I was glad I didn't because I knew I would want to play that Ken had come over and started kicking.

The next day, the woman visited, and I saw a real-life black eye. "Why does she even have a boyfriend?" I wondered. My only information about boyfriends and girlfriends came from Barbie commercials on Saturday mornings. I liked having women in our home, but I worried. What if the boyfriends got mad that we were helping the girls and came to stop us? What if these men found my house? What if they kicked my mom? I was always afraid that something bad would happen to her, but she kept helping.

The scariness of it all dawned on me that day. Hot tingling had always crawled up my neck in those situations, but I usually tried not to think about it and focused on the important work I was helping mom do. I believed she was an awesome hero, and I always will. But after the stomach kicking, I felt responsible for being a hero too. The firstborn sense of responsibility to mother my mother rose to the surface of my consciousness. I became preoccupied with reading my mom's mood.

"Are you mad at me?" I'd ask.

"No. I'm just tired," she'd say, and I'm sure she was. I still wondered, though, and kept asking. The exchange became a little call and response routine that we rehearsed every day. Sometimes I'd ask if she was "sad at me" instead. I developed a mix of independence and drama. I didn't want to be a problem for her, but then I also wanted to get more attention and would over-dramatize things. I'd keep to myself the real, big things like lying awake terrified every night that someone would come to hurt my mother, but I'd throw fits about petty things. Then I would feel ashamed for acting out because how could my problems ever rate against that grown-up stuff? The needs constantly warred in my little head and body: attention versus accommodation.

Once, Dad came home after an allergy shot dose increase and began slipping into anaphylactic shock. I remember him going to the car as my mom said, "Jessica, just wait here and be still. Grammy will be here soon." She pulled the front door shut, and I watched through the big picture window as they pulled back into the street and sped away. I vaguely understood that my dad could die and fully grasped that at age four I was too little to be home alone. I panicked. We had a blue couch with little red flowers and an old, rustic coffee table with an ancient piece of Big Red tacked to the bottom. I buried my face in the couch but then was overwhelmed by the volcano of fear in my little body. I jumped up and ran laps around the coffee table, screaming, crying, and pulling the curls around my face.

Within only a minute or two, my grandmother's gold Lincoln pulled up between the two old elm trees near the curb. I stopped running and turned away from the window to drag my sleeves across my cheeks. I can't be sure what words I used as I scolded myself, but I remember the sentiment: "What an idiot, running around like a baby for no reason." When Grammy came to the door, I let her in and behaved as if everything was business as usual. I didn't want to be a problem. Why should I be crying? Daddy was the one who could die.

I don't remember any time when I wasn't preoccupied with perception. I wanted so badly for everyone to see the good things I did and turned into one of those kids who is always saying, "I know all my times tables perfectly" or "I got put in the special reading group." Meanwhile, I felt like a screw-up. I often couldn't control my temper, and those constant grabs for attention could backfire. Most Texans don't like a show-offy child.

My parents loved me, though, deeply and clearly. I never wondered whether or not they wanted me.

* * *

Mom put me in a ballet class, and it hooked me forever. Theatrical and cute in a leotard, I was natural and joyful when I danced. All my look-at-me found the perfect excuses: I can do the splits! I can do ballet!

Recitals meant real stages and permission to show off. I started with a jazz/ballet combo with blonde Miss Sharon in 1987. She played scratchy records with song lyrics like: *Tendue. Tendue. We love to do tendue.* It's strange to think of a time when I didn't yet know the vocabulary, when *plié, relevé,* and *tendue* were still Greek to me or, rather, French. This head now rattles with French verbs.

Teachers always said to go home and practice, so I did. I didn't know I was probably the only one and practiced a lot. Dancing alone in my backyard, dodging dog piles and staining my heels and knees grass green left me floating for a while.

All those little courses at the Amarillo College set me up for a dancing future. I wasn't screaming and begging to be taken home like some kids. I felt early on that this was serious work. "WE LOVE TO DO TENDUE. No messing around. People want to see some serious ballet performance. And I'm going to give it to them." I never suffered from stage fright. The teachers were kind and sweet to us, which was good since the next teacher took a very different tack.

* * *

When I turned seven, we decided to choose a new dance school. Somehow I learned to be judgmental early. One school wasn't legit at all—Miss Dee taught baton twirling, for gosh sake. But then there was the Hess School of Dance, a tough and wonderful place.

During my first class at this *real* ballet school, I felt a new cocktail of chemicals coursing through me every few minutes. Fear! Elation! Fear! Elation! My mom had told me, "Mrs. Hess is strict." Turns out, at Hess School of Dance "strict" was a respectful word for terrifyingly mean.

For weeks, I fantasized over the class. Now in the studio, the starry-eyed dreaminess I generated laid a ballerina over the mirror image of my scrawny body. My imagination distracted me from reality, and Mrs. Hess was not pleased. The humming joy coming off of my buzzing, electrified little nervous system plugged my ears. I kept coming-to with the sounds of the music starting or a harsh word, but then I would sink back into imagining that the gawky Bambi in the mirror was already a star.

Mrs. Hess's Bostonian cackle of a voice snapped me back with the sharpness of a thick rubber band against my skin. "GET over here! Turn AROUND! NOT THAT WAY!" Thankfully, my fluffy, warm fuzziness created by the hopes of my heart protected me from the sting that day. I felt Mrs. Hess's disgust with me and could tell that I was doing it all wrong. But I could only hear, "I'm a ballerina!" My own positivity bug-zapped each biting word from Mrs. Hess.

HESS SCHOOL OF DANCE

The more life you had, the more the base expanded,
so that the wounds and treasons that were nearly imperceptible
when they happened stretched like tiny dots on a balloon
slowly blown up. A speck on the slender child grows into a gross
deformity in the adult, inescapable, ragged at the edges.

Lauren Groff
Fates and Furies

The dance school looked like a low, flat, ugly house, but inside there were only four sections. Two long, narrow studios divided by a center wall connected via doors at either end. One was smaller than the other because the cramped, red-linoleum lobby area took up the extra space. A closet-sized bathroom that always smelled of urine and Pinesol was in the far corner of the lobby space. The entry served as a kind of holding area for the little dancers waiting for class to begin, and it was invisibly but strictly divided into hierarchical sections.

The older dancers sat in the center. Big girls like them, the ones who needed to tape their toes and put on "toe shoes" before class, didn't arrive until the 5:15 class. The younger, 4:15 kids would sit there, but there was an inscrutable rule about who was allowed. On my first day at the Hess School of Dance, I decided to work my way into that prime pre-class real estate.

Sometimes the pay phone installed just to the right of the entrance, across the room from the bathroom would ring, and the girls would all jump up. "I'll get it!" Laser-eyed looks would shoot out from a few queen bees to subdue the misfits; then the queens would dive to see who could get to it first. "Hess School of Dance," they would squeak, trying to sound older than they were.

In those very first weeks at the Hess School of Dance, I saw an opportunity to have some control and social success. I thought maybe the dance school would be a place where I could clearly know my place in comparison to my peers. Maybe, I hoped, I could make Mrs. Hess happy.

Around the time I started with the Hesses, I began exclusively homeschooling. The requirement to please my mother academically added another dimension to our relationship. And I was lonely, very lonely.

I figured I could make friends and a place for myself at ballet. I often questioned whether I would ever be good enough. Good enough to solve my mother's fatigue, good enough to be allowed to go back to school with all the other kids, good enough to have a sense of peace and completion. I wonder whether some of us are just born trying to be the best, needing everyone to be happy with us. I hoped the ballet studio, where I felt happy and engaged, would be a place I found success and self-satisfaction.

CAMILLE

What if to love and be loved's not enough?
What if I fall and can't bear to get up?
Oh, I wish, for once, we could stay gold

First Aid Kit
"Stay Gold" from *Stay Gold*

I cannot imagine what would have happened if I had called her "Camille." She was and forever will be "Mrs. Hess." Roald Dahl would have put her in *The Witches*.

Mrs. Hess could command the attention of a hundred shrinking adults, though she was only 5' 3" and was hobbled by old injuries. She had no qualms destroying card houses of confidence with her smash of a sneer or mockery. She wore bright lipstick and had a distinct nose. Her hair functioned, we decided, as DEFCON warning system: ponytail on average mood days, half up with curls on good days, and tightly wound foam rollers on especially mean days. Our sweet Texas drawls were no match for her East Coast accent. She was capricious, but like only children can, we hoped against hope that she would be more fun than scary on any given day.

We were fat. We were garbage. We were dancing like dead fish. We were stupid. We were lazy. We were obviously not right in our minds. We were dull. We were selfish. We were wasting her time. We would never amount to anything. We were slobs. We were rarely even called by the correct names. Heaven help us if we were late! I don't think I've been late for anything since about 1988; it's now metaphysically impossible.

All that to say: she was a town treasure. We loved ballet, and she held the keys.

Theoretically, the psychological state of fear and anxiety she induced should not have been conducive for learning. She could not demonstrate much. She had old injuries and limitations, but she could show us arm, head, and shoulder movements. There was a lovely quality to her *epaulement* (the way a dancer uses her chest and collar bone). Somehow her words and scoffing would eventually communicate whatever new step she was teaching us. I have a very detailed recollection of the afternoon that we learned *tour jetes*. It was like playing some kind of full-body guessing game. As a dance instructor, I can say that teaching *tour jetes* for the first time is hard enough when there is a demonstrator! We all wanted to figure it out for her, though. We wanted so, so badly for her to say, "YES! That's it. Good girl." Oh, how we longed for her praise!

Toward the end of the year when we were working on recital dances, we would begin the dreaded contests. There were usually two classes in session during any time slot. The other class was taught by an assistant teacher. During the last twenty minutes of class, we would combine to watch each others' dances. At the end, we would line up shoulder to shoulder, facing the mirror. Mrs. Hess would march along and hold her hand above each girl's head one by one. Those seated with backs against the mirror were meant to clap for the one/s we thought did the best.

Some girls got no clapping. If we clapped for someone who was bad or didn't keep up, Mrs. Hess would scold us. Some girls got a few claps from the nice kids in the other class. One or two girls, Mrs. Hess's pets, got all the applause. I did eventually become a pet, but even when I reached the level of winning contests I felt this terrible mix of thrill and guilt. I felt so bad for the other girls. I always wondered, "Why do you come?!" Winners got an extra piece of candy. I think that my unnatural love for mellowcreme pumpkins (as evidenced by The Great Halloween Candy Binge of 2001) is a side effect of surviving Mrs. Hess. Candy was the taste of her approval. Now, I don't much like the stuff.

I remember being hit on my butt a few times, like a spank almost, but it was done in the way one might smack at an animal that wasn't in the right place. Mostly, the physical stuff came in the form of pinches and pokes from her fingernails. Sometimes it was hair-pulling. She'd grab you by the bun and yank you into position or pull your face back to yell into it. I believed she was mean, but I also believed that if we could all just do it right and quit screwing up all the time she'd be fine and nice.

She respected hard work, and that suited me fine. I did not have to be asked to work hard at ballet. I was always ready for class on time. My parents and I have no recollection of my needing to be dragged or begged. I quickly saw that coming early, staying late, keeping your mouth shut, and staying out of her way were the keys to the success and approval I craved. I loved to ask her about famous ballerinas. She told us how Carla Fracci would dance like an angel on stage then run off to heave and curse in the wings, swearing never to dance again. At those times, there was a hint of fun in the studio.

I dreamed of having my picture on the studio wall like one of her beautiful, New York City Ballet ballerina daughters. The youngest was named Alexia, a must-have name for any aspiring ballet dancer. I would always be "Alexia" in my playtime fantasies. Mrs. Hess definitely succeeded in communicating a goal: dance in a ballet company. I can thank her for that, though I remained fuzzy for some time as to how one would actually get to such heights from Amarillo. Come to think of it, Mrs. Hess rarely talked to any of us like we could or would be ballerinas some day. All her grand illustrations seemed to be more for the purpose of showing us what we were not. I guess it's good, then, that I was daft enough to have dreams of getting there anyway.

When I was ten, my mom suggested that next time Mrs. Hess corrected me I thank her. I waited for an opportunity. When she yelled at me about something, I practiced whatever it was for a second after the curtsey and candy line then stepped up to her and said, "Thanks for helping me."

"For WHAT?"

"Helping me with that [whatever it was]; I think I under-stand now."

She was taken aback: "Oh... well, you're welcome." I'm pretty certain that's when things started to change for me. I decided right then that I wanted her to speak like that to me instead, so I worked even harder and asked even more questions.

I crossed some unconscionable line at times, but I soon became skilled at reading her. I can see a hurt feeling, anger, or admiration from a mile away, no matter how hard someone is trying to hide it. I learned how to make Mrs. Hess happy with me. I learned the benefits of loyalty. She began to confide in me. She'd tell me ahead of time what we were going to do that day. She'd have me help with the younger students. Once she even brought me a box of her daughters' old clothes and leotards. I was willing to do just about anything to stay in her good graces, so I worked harder than ever.

At the end of the day, what mattered to her was how I made

her feel and how I made her look. She'd trash me in a heartbeat if I embarrassed her (in her imagination) by making a mistake in a performance or in class. But at least she was invested in me. She began to drop hints as to how I would actually become a dancer. When I would succeed, she would say so, and that felt incredible.

In one final dress rehearsal of *The Nutcracker* my junior year, she made a point to tell me how breathtaking a particular moment of my "Snow Queen" *pas de deux* was. I was so proud. My partner and I had been working tirelessly on the backward leap and catch, a "flying fish." Earlier that day, the conductor of the Amarillo Symphony Orchestra tracked me down to tell me the same thing. He even used the same word: "breathtaking." A crowning moment! I did something right!

In the next act, I danced "Sugar Plum Fairy." Two leads in one show is a rough bill. I was exhausted by the end and had one minute to breathe before going back out for the finale. I dared to sit, boldly committing a heinous sin. We were strictly warned throughout our lives at the Hess School of Dance to NEVER, EVER sit in a costume. Mrs. Hess burst through the curtain of my dressing room, and said, "There you are. I knew it! Don't be so lazy! You are destroying that costume! A thread was hanging the whole time! How dare you treat these costumes that way!?"

I jumped up and apologized, but I thought to myself, "How dare you treat *people* this way?" The thought passed quickly, though. I was accustomed to being treated like a dancer.

NEIL

If you wanted the sky I would write across the sky in letters
That would soar a thousand feet high "To Sir, With Love"

Don Black and Mark London
To Sir with Love

Until age eleven the only exposure girls had to MISTER Hess came with *The Nutcracker* or jazz choreography time. Hess Jazz was a genre unto itself, truly unlike anything I learned later. The pop song to back us up had always been off the music charts for at least ten years. The movements were all done in one place, more like semaphore than Fosse. But we didn't know anything different at the time, and his presence meant a break from Mrs. Hess.

Mr. Neil Hess had begun his career in Amarillo as the drama teacher and director at Tascosa High School. By the time

I was his student, he was the director of our local ballet company, the Lone Star Ballet, dance director of the West Texas State University (later to become West Texas A&M, WTAMU), and the teacher for the older dancers at the Hess School of Dance. The day you graduated to Mr. Hess's 5:15 class was a special day. He could get angry and frustrated, but it was at a normal level; nothing like his wife. He gave quirky combinations at the barre. Typical exercises would be punctuated by strange arm waving or even tap dancing. We never did anything once but always at least four or five times. His most common comments and corrections included, "heel forward," "chin back," and "chest up." All great advice, and if I teach, those are things I say the most too (along with "straighten your knees!").

Beyond the dance instruction, though, Mr. Hess was a consummate teacher. He constantly spoke about life, art, and beauty. He had the skill and knowledge to teach us dance steps and choreography, but his ability to inspire made him a treasure. (Or: *TRAYsure*, as he pronounced it.) At least once per class but usually more times, he would stop the music, stare into space and begin, "You know, dancers...." Sometimes he called us "people," as in, "People, you need to know...." What followed emphasized the failing state of human hearts and the power of art and religion to revive them. He taught us that what we were doing was much, much more than entertaining. Art and beauty, according to Mr. Hess, lifted the spirit and inspired people to be better spiritually and morally. Without ever citing research, he convinced us that children and adults exposed to the arts, particularly dance training, were smarter and quicker to learn any other discipline. He yearned for dance to receive the kind of attention given mostly to sports in our country. (Mrs. Hess called girls who were caught playing sports "ball-pushers," and they were supposedly kicked out of the school.)

During all the soap-boxing, two things were bound to happen: the retucking of his belly into his pants and the drawing of a comb from his pocket and across the front part of his hairdo. Once on a tour, he was yelling at us and backed himself right off the edge of the stage. We were all mortified, but thankfully the elementary school stage did not have an orchestra pit. Mr. Hess popped up quickly, and the comb immediately emerged. "Just keep dancing," he said. "That is what is important."

As I grew older, I joined the ranks of those Mr. Hess would regularly ask to demonstrate combinations during the class. "Jessica, do it," he'd say, and he would start the music. Everyone would clap when I finished; that was the unspoken rule. We'd all smile with congratulations to girls asked to demonstrate for the first time. His feedback was never insulting or useless. Even his teasing was kind. We all dreaded the possibility of being zoned out when he wanted our attention because he would whistle as to a dog until he got it. I remember it happening to me once, and I blushed with shame even as I had to chuckle with everyone else.

When I was fourteen, Mr. Hess saw me as promising and began giving me private lectures. Where Mrs. Hess had issued the challenge: "I dare you to be good enough," Mr. Hess invited me to transcend human nature and become an artist, a priest who brings healing beauty to the world and represents the better aspects of my kin. I needed and wanted to believe that art really was all he claimed it was. I wanted the sad to be healed and the pained to be comforted.

Many times, everyone else would be gone, and my mom or dad would come in looking for me. Mr. Hess would say, "Hello. We were just talking about how to be a dancer" or something like that, and my mom or dad would say, "Well, thank you." I always felt safe around him and wildly lucky that he was willing to instruct me about auditioning, navigating the rich girls who were jealous, and conducting myself like an artist, a professional. "Watch," he always said. "If you see something beautiful, try to understand why it works."

During *The Nutcracker* rehearsals and performances every

year, we spent time with "the college kids." I did my first performance in 1990. Seeing how Mr. Hess treated them made me
want to spend even more time dancing for him. He kept a
Junior Company, a small group of younger dancers who would
perform with the Lone Star Ballet. They were the JV. I always
wanted to be in that group, and when I was first invited to go
down to the college for Junior Company rehearsals, I spent half
an hour on my hair.

At the college studio, I heard more speeches. Even though
the college dancers often made fun of Mr. Hess, they too loved
him deeply. And he loved them back. Any success that a former
student had was trumpeted to us all the moment he got the call
or the letter.

I wanted to make him proud and to give him stories to tell
about me.

THE NUTCRACKER

MARCH 2, 3, 4, 5, 6,
POINT! BOW!
MARCH 2, 3, 4, 5, 6
POINT! BOW!
Chassé, chassé, chassé, chassé, chassé, chassé
POINT! BOW!

Camille Hess
"Party Scene" from *The Nutcracker*

I was cast at age seven in a role that made me the very first body on the stage, a little "party girl" on her way to Clara's house. I learned this at my first ever *Nutcracker* rehearsal. When the steps were shown to me by Mrs. Hess and another little girl, I got nervous and said that I wasn't sure I could do it. Mrs. Hess was disgusted. She raised her eyebrows through the roof and sarcastically said, "Oh, so you don't want to do it? Fine then. Why don't you just sit down if this is all too hard for you." I had no idea what to do. Clearly this was a trap. To sit would be wrong, but to keep trying felt impossible. I froze and said nothing until she screamed, "Just get out of the way!"

My mother rescued me by calling Mr. Hess to complain about the unfair treatment. Mrs. Hess had essentially kicked me out of the production for that moment of childish nerves. I went to the next rehearsal and was re-taught the steps that had frightened me. I never complained again and learned that I could indeed do hard things. I also learned that expressing fear was a huge mistake, and I decided that I should keep my fears to myself through the remainder of my time at the Hess School of Dance.

That same Christmas, Mrs. Hess screamed at my mother for wanting to help with our class Christmas party. Mom was terribly upset and offended, and I dreaded the possibility that I'd be taken out of the school. I pulled out my brand new diary, the present I had taken from the pile in the gift exchange at the party. I drew the very best picture I could. It was a close-up of a little girl's face with a giant tear falling down the cheek. I wrote an entry about how trapped I felt between pleasing Mrs. Hess and protecting my family. It's no wonder that I downplayed to my mom the screaming and pinching I experienced at the Hess School of Dance. I needed both women so badly, needed their approval to feel right in my own skin.

After months of rehearsals, we finally went to the theater. It was only the Amarillo Civic Center Auditorium but may as well have been Radio City. I walked into the house for the first big cast meeting. The audience seats seemed to go on forever. I saw real scenery for the first time. The beauty and magnitude were overwhelming. I could never have pictured it if anyone had tried to explain it. And, oh, that smell! The theater set for a ballet smells like curling iron and painted canvas, and it's the best smell in the world after french fries. The older girls acted like it was perfectly normal and were trying to be cool. But I gawked endlessly. We sat in the house seats, and Mr. Hess used a microphone to talk to us. He said "People" to us a lot. I felt the magic and seriousness of work in the theater. The first day in a theater for every show I did after that held the same buzz of joy, an anticipatory energy.

For *The Nutcracker*, kids and parents endured the spikey parts of Mrs. Hess. Our Lone Star Ballet production boasted incredible sets, costumes, special effects, and even real professional dancers who came to dance Sugar Plum Fairy and Cavalier. Most students, but not everyone, danced at least something in the show. There was a hierarchy. To be Clara was the best, party girl next, then soldier, then mouse. Many of us did more than one part, sometimes many more.

The Nutcracker is training tool, civic holiday treasure, and cash cow all in one. Think about it: How might we get more people to come to the ballet? Put their kids in it! Make it a holiday tradition! Most major ballet companies do twenty or more performances of it. That's a lot of income and minimal new expense. Outside of *The Nutcracker* and a few other beloved ballets, companies attract audiences with new work or with refurbishments. New Scenery! New Effects! New Choreography! New! New! New! The arts in the United States are as subject to consumerism as every other industry.

Little ballet students know nothing of those facts of life. They only know that *The Nutcracker* gets them into real costumes, real moments on stage, and real applause. It also conveniently supplies a visible ladder to climb. Students can go from Mother Ginger Buffoon, to Party Girl, to Fairy, to Chinese, to Flower, to Snowflake, to Mirliton, to Arabian, to Dew Drop, to Snow Queen, to Sugar Plum Friggin' Fairy. Human Resource Managers will tell you about factors of job satisfaction: meaningful work, adequate compensation, and room for advancement. *The Nutcracker* supplies all these things for the smallest of ballet schools and world-renowned companies.

I would have given up sugar and gifts for the rest of my life just to dance *The Nutcracker* each year. I once received a snow globe with a Clara teddy bear in it from my on-stage Party Scene "mother." I would hide between my lit Christmas tree and the wall of our living room and wish as hard as I could that with the flip of the snow globe I would become the real Clara and be taken away to a world where I could dance forever. I never was cast as Clara, but I danced every other part I could ever want. The Lone Star Ballet satisfied with chances to dance Dew Drop Fairy, Snow Queen, and even the Sugar Plum Fairy.

Real ballerinas came from New York to dance with us. Before I even understood what I was doing, I found myself in lines with all my little friends asking for autographs from the stars on my ballet slippers. We would ask the visiting Sugar Plum if we could please have a pointe shoe. I don't think I ever received one, but I treasured the signatures on the soles of my shoes from New Yorkers like Alexia herself and Peter Boal.

Our time together backstage was precious. All the friends and moms settled in for the week, creating a type of tent city that consisted of makeup mirrors, Caboodles, and costume racks. We spread blankets and coats to play on while we waited. I can still remember the soft, warm feeling of my mother's fingertips patting and smoothing makeup onto my face. She was the perfect "stage mom" because she never got sucked into any drama and was in no way after her own glory. It was a bonus that she was great at makeup, hair, and whatever crafting or sewing was required.

I was sixteen when I danced one show of Sugar Plum before our guest artists arrived. The week before a high fever and strep throat ravaged my overtired body, and I was barely recovered for theater week. I remember rasping to Jerry, my partner, halfway through the *pas de deux*, "think happy thoughts for me." He gave me a squeeze on my hand; we rallied together and finished strong. There is nothing, NOTHING like the second wind that comes with powerful music or audience applause. My physician came the next day to opening night to see my Snow Queen. He said, "I don't think you should dance, but if you're going to do it anyway, I'd like to see" and sat in the front row. It went perfectly.

The Nutcracker became as essential to Christmas as the tree, lights, cookies, everything. I knew what Christmas was all about, Charlie Brown, but a nutcracker lurked just outside that stable door, clacking those wooden teeth.

TEXAS

We invite you all to come to Texas
We expect you all to come to Texas!

Paul Green
"Texas" from *TEXAS*

Around the edge of Amarillo, the land is terraced and stepped. Prickly pear cacti dot the landscape. Scrubby 100-year-old mesquite trees look both perfect and out of place in the fields. The sky is in such plain view that city people may even find it indecent. Some people swear you can tell a storm is coming by how the cows group together. When there's a storm, you can hardly break away from watching, even in the face of danger. Dad once nearly had his perfect Kansas City-style, grilled ribs ruined by an incoming tornado and the accompaniment of softball-sized hail. Fortunately, we got the ribs off and enjoyed them without any concussions.

Our own precious canyon, the Palo Duro, boasts being the

second largest canyon in the United States, the "Grand Canyon of Texas." I've seen the Grand Canyon, and I can confidently say the PDC lives up to its moniker. The entrance to the canyon is a forty-minute drive from Amarillo. We would go there for field trips, barbeques, and camping. It is a feast for the eyes and a treasure trove for any rock or fossil hound. On an off-trail hike with my dad, we once found a fossil the shape and size of a bull's horn. A professor from WTAMU told Dad that it's likely a sloth toe bone, but I think it's an iguanadon thumb myself. My favorite fossils to find are seashells and coral; imagining that place full of water makes me feel small and temporary.

The other claim to fame for the Palo Duro Canyon is the Pioneer Amphitheater and its resident production, *TEXAS,* a musical drama that tells the stories of early Texas Panhandle settlers, both farmers and cattlemen. I have no idea what the national impression of *TEXAS* is, but I do know that locally it is treasured. To me, it might as well have been *The Lion King* or *Phantom of the Opera.* I knew many of the performers because the show was mostly cast with members of the West Texas A&M dance, music, and theater departments, and Mr. Hess was the director. Lucky for me, my dad's band was the pre-show entertainment on the weekends. The Prairie Dogs are a group of buddies who still play music together for fun. I love each one of them like an uncle (or Dad!).

From age seven until I was a teenager my Saturday evenings every summer were spent in the canyon running amok with all the other little band kids. A small, easily scaled mesa stood above the gift shop and barbeque area. It was our wonderland. We named every crevice and boulder, knew every hidey-hole and bluff, all the different routes for going up or down. Being little Panhandle kids, we knew how to watch out for snakes and what to do if and when we found them. Sometimes our pockets and fanny packs jangled with allowance money to buy trinkets, cap guns, and rock candy from the gift shop that smelled like all the cedar kitsch it contained. I still wish I had bought a coaster with the words "Round Tuit" burned into its center. But I never got around to it.

My favorite thing to do, though I wasn't bold enough to do it often, was to beg barbeque off the caterer who sold styrofoam plates loaded with deliciousness to the droves of visitors who came on tour buses. Slow-smoked barbeque beef and sausage, potato salad, coleslaw, soupy "ranch-style" beans, thick white bread with preserved apricot topping, sliced sweet onions, and hamburger dill pickles. Sometimes when the line died down and food was left over, Joey, the proprietor, would let us get a twenty-ounce styrofoam cup and fill it with whatever we wanted. I have put away more potato salad in my day than anyone I know. I'm sure of it.

Another favorite pastime at "the play *TEXAS*" was star-watching. Like a Hollywood tourist, I would camp out and wait to catch sight of Mr. Hess or any of his dancers. These were the only professional dancers I knew, and I could not wait to join them. One asked me to wish her "*merde*," and so I learned the common good luck charm among dancers. Sometimes I would sneak to the top of the amphitheater to watch the opening number while my dad and his bandmates packed up their equipment and then ate the plates of barbecue Joey had saved for them. I loved everything about what I was seeing, every time. I learned the choreography and would show it off to the dancers whenever I had a chance.

The dancers' life seemed to be a great one. They spent every night in my favorite place. Joey treated them like movie stars. Little kids camped out just to get a look, and crowds of people waited with excitement just to sit and watch them show off.

ELISE

At the Hess School of Dance there were no classes during the summer. We were strongly encouraged to attend the West Texas State University Dance Camp. I begged my parents to be allowed to go. Mr. Hess gave me scholarships the years we could not afford it. The first year I went I was ten years old, the youngest student staying in the dorms. Camp was run and taught by Dance Department majors, and it was a blast. We took classes in genres that I did not often get to explore: tap, jazz (real jazz... not the stuff Mr. Hess choreographed for us), musical theater, and modern dance. I learned a great deal, but mostly I learned that there were teachers and dancers in the world who were kind and encouraging. It was then that I started to understand that my body was made for dance, that I was more flexible than everyone else.

We would be sleeping away from home in the WTAMU dorms for six nights, and I was nervous. Getting settled that first afternoon, I bid my fears goodbye when I laid eyes on Elise Carlton. She was a few years older than me, blue-eyed, blonde, and always smiling. She tucked me under her wing and gave me a cup of puffed cheese balls, assuring me and my parents that I would be fine.

Elise was a star at the studio during the year. I first met her when I was seven, during that first *Nutcracker*. I was terribly nervous then too, and Elise had the same effect: calming encouragement. Elise had been splitting the starring role of Clara with another girl named Tanny. On opening night, all the cast members exchanged gifts, little cookies, ornaments, or trinkets. I got a little nutcracker soldier whose arms and legs flailed when you pulled the string. The foot has a little inscription: "Elise Carlton 1990."

Even at seven, I could gather that some mommies gave lots of money to the ballet, some didn't, and some would have if they could. There was a definite presence of Texan socialites in the arts scene. My mother joined the Lone Star Ballet Guild because it seemed like the right thing to do, but she wasn't really into the club aspect of it all. Now, I'm not saying that the ONLY reason girls got to be Clara was because of money. In later years some of those rich girls were also my friends, were mostly kind, and were talented. I am saying that having your mother be active in the Guild and high up on the donation list weren't bad things. Perhaps my childhood impressions and recollections aren't right. Elise had a lovely mom, but she didn't seem to be too into the club thing either.

Elise, so beautiful and talented, had one of the best attitudes I've ever seen. She was a perfect Clara. I can still see her lovely little arabesque turn in the second act with her long, blonde, perfect sausage curls swinging out behind her. The blue of her bow complimenting her natural coloring perfectly, she was a Renoir or Cassat.

At camp I got to know Elise even better. She was hilarious and suffered no fools; mean girls didn't stand a chance around Elise. She once burped the most awful burp I've ever heard, and I will never forget it. The grossness made her human and brave. To be that unladylike without shame? Unheard of.

I marveled that she and her friends let me be a part of their crew. One, Flannery, was an absolute beauty with thick, dirty blonde hair and big blue eyes. I have a picture of her holding up a magazine cover graced with Niki Taylor next to her own face, a dead ringer at age thirteen. I felt like such a fuzzy-headed, gangly goofball next to them all.

While Elise and her friends earned driver's licenses and went to the prom, I was taking extra dance classes and eventually passed them on the dance ladder. Dance became their extracurricular while I danced seven or more hours a day. But Elise's behavior was proof to me that there was more to being successful than raw talent and hard work alone; attitude really mattered. I wanted the same confident kindness as Elise, which made such a difference to our whole school. Mrs. Hess was mean to Elise and her friends too; no one escaped that. But Elise almost did.

When Elise graduated from high school, she worked for *TEXAS* down in the canyon. She wasn't the star of the show—perhaps she was no longer interested in spending hours on dancing—but she was using her five-star smile as a member of the hospitality team. I saw her there a few times, and it was always such a joyful conversation. I can still see her in the awful, ruffle-necked, gingham-checked dresses all the women on hospitality had to wear.

Later that summer, while I was at ballet camp, my dad

called to let me know that Elise had died in a car accident between the canyon and Amarillo. She was only nineteen. The ornament from 1990 has been given a place of honor on every Christmas tree since then.

SUNDAY SCHOOL ANSWERS

You gotta know who to
Who to listen to

Amy Grant
"Who To Listen To" from *Unguarded*

I think Elise was a Christian, like most of the people I knew in Amarillo. But she didn't talk about it. Her kindness and goodness weren't rooted in religiosity, and that intrigued me. I had always believed in God because I had no reason not to. I found comfort in all the confident facts I had been taught; I liked having a sense that any existential question I had could probably be answered. It wasn't until years later that I realized thinking one has all the answers can be more of a problem than solution.

Back then I hated being pressed to talk about my "relationship with Jesus." I didn't have one, but I hid that fact by knowing how to answer all the questions I was asked about him. The denomination in which I was raised is often criticized for overemphasizing intellectual arguments for the Christian faith and neglecting personal transformation, emotion, and relationship. I'm sure that tone both aided and excused my unwillingness to really investigate Jesus on an emotional, personal level.

My relationship to our church and to Christian faith was tricky and immature. On one hand, it provided a way to be successful and impress adults. Memorization of catechism and Scripture was easy for me. I was bright and could easily follow theological concepts and arguments; I loved answering questions. Staying engaged during classes and worship pleased the grownups. I wasn't dishonest in my answers; I never said things I didn't believe. But I tended to focus more on staying "right" with the adults and with God rather than finding out who God really was and what he was like. I think that's often how faith begins with children.

I was glad my parents believed someone was watching over us all, over them. My mom spoke about Jesus with a power and genuineness I could not ignore. She told incredible stories about God reaching out to her. Once as a twelve-year-old, she heard a praise song she liked at camp. Later walking along in a park, she prayed a simple request. "God, if you help me remember those words, I can sing that song to you." She stopped in her tracks, and at her feet was a folded piece of paper. It had the whole song written on it in pencil.

I saw the paper. It's practically a relic in my mind, like something Jesus touched.

She seemed most confident and reassured when she spoke about Jesus. I did not feel the way she did about him, but I could see that he had a real effect on her. Her personal, tangible stories forced me to consider that this larger story I was told was probably true.

I had yet to feel God in any extraordinary way myself, but I assented to everything I was taught. I had moments of doubt. I remember a season of intensely worrying that maybe God really was evil and somehow managed to convince everyone that he was good. But, like most of my other big questions and concerns, that fear faded with the progression of daily life. Sunday school answers to my questions sufficed, and I figured that someday I would have a more sure faith and the peace and joy I was promised.

INDEPENDENCE

To sing, to laugh, to dream, to walk in my own way and be alone,
free, with an eye to see things as they are...
To travel any road under the sun, under the stars, nor doubt
if fame or fortune lie beyond the bourne—

Edmund Rostand
Cyrano de Bergerac

I skipped the eighth grade as a homeschooler so I could attend classes at a specialty math and science school run by our public school system, the Amarillo Area Center for Advanced Learning (AACAL). I wanted to be a doctor, cardiologist specifically. I made choices to impress and to live up to the potential I knew I had. My parents' friends seemed to love hearing me explain cardiology. I was thrilled to the gills to get to go to real school!

Ballet was still my after-school activity. At dance, I felt most challenged and the most pleasure, but I still didn't exactly understand how one would have a life in dance. So I was going to be a doctor. I was a big dork at the magnet school: one or two years younger than the other kids, the only one who had been homeschooled, and still losing teeth. I remember being teased for wearing my dad's old letter jacket which I thought was cool. I somehow managed to make friends though. We had a great time competing in medical spelling and biomedical debate at our Health Occupation Students of America competitions.

The main things I learned at AACAL were how to look like I was actually smoking a cigarette and how to casually drop a curse word or two. I think I was trying to make up for the gapped smile and biomedical spelling bees. I recall staring into the mirror in my bathroom mouthing the "f" word to practice. I never got in trouble for these activities, though I was nearly caught several times. It was easy to talk my way out, being the ace student and innocent homeschooler that I was. But after six weeks of fake-smoking cigarettes, conviction racked my tiny bones. Hours after bedtime, I confessed to my mother in a tell-all expose of my newfound bad-assery.

I swore to never do it again, and I didn't. Though I did drink half a wine cooler or two at some dancer parties a couple years later. That was the extent of my wild years.

I don't think my parents were thrilled with AACAL, and it began to lose its luster for me too. By that point, thanks to the arrival of some dancers from another town, I knew what I had to do if I was going to actually make good on becoming a ballerina when I grew up. I needed to go to training workshops at big ballet schools and companies in the summer and dance A LOT. Finally, homeschooling held attraction for me.

My parents and Mr. Hess talked, and I got myself the deal I wanted. The classes and rehearsals that I committed to at the West Texas A&M Dance Department were a lot of work, but it felt like heaven to me.

I belonged! No one thought I was lame! Mr. Hess let me join the Lone Star Ballet, my dream team. To my delight and surprise, I found affection there. I've not had better hugs in my life than the tight, lift-me-off-my-tippy-toes embraces of my male dancing partners. To my great joy, every day they kissed my cheeks, braided my hair, and waltzed me around the room. These people got it: stage love, look-at-me syndrome, get-me-out-of-Texas, all of it. There was zero judgment from my fellow dancers. They were cheerful and proud of me.

For a year and a half, my family had to drive me back and forth to the university in Canyon twice a day on weekdays and once on Saturdays and Sundays. My poor little sister lived much of her life in the back seat of my mom's car waiting for me to get out of ballet. I especially loved when my dad would come pick me up at night. We didn't get to see each other very much because we both worked a lot. I loved trying to convince him to drive through a fast food place. Once, we each got about halfway through our McDonald's cheeseburgers and halfway back to Amarillo before we realized they hadn't put any meat on them. Delicious.

At 16, after Mom's white knuckles had the blood run back to them, a driver's license settled in my wallet. I looked great in my license photograph—tan, wearing a cerulean blue scoop neck t-shirt, made up with silver eyeliner I borrowed from my grandmother's makeup stash and shimmering lipstick. Even at the time I thought it was a good picture, which is saying something.

That license was the ticket to a new chapter in my life. I kept the windows down in my red Saturn station wagon and the radio up. I was tuned to what was happening in indie music and worked hard to learn the names of all the songs and bands I liked. We had two absolutely fantastic college radio stations, and I had them on every possible second. When I did my school work in the mornings (alone), I would keep the clock radio on my desk playing very quietly. If my mom came in to check on me, I would reach for the eraser that I had strategically placed on the snooze button and turn it off. My goal was to get all my favorite songs recorded on my stash of mix-tapes.

At night, I would listen to our local NPR station and began my lifelong love for public radio.

Each day I would blow through my school work as quickly as I could. "Yeah, yeah, yeah: math, history, science. I get it. Get me out of here." It wasn't that I didn't like academics. I at least *wanted* to be smart and well-read, but I loved being with people and working on dancing so very much. I was red-blooded and alive in the studio. At 11:40 a.m. each school day it was finally time to get in my car and leave.

That twenty-minute drive was such a happy part of my day. I felt like myself. I wasn't a loser trying to fit in at the magnet school (even if my last tooth had finally grown in!). I wasn't afraid of failure or disappointment. I had managed not to get in trouble badly enough to earn the no-ballet punishment that was always threatened. I was wearing lots and lots of lipstick and dangly earrings. I listened to my loud music and dreamed about all the dancing to come.

My best friends were at the college, and Aaron was my very bestie, my partner in learning about the professional ballet world. (Also I was madly in love with him and in complete denial that he liked boys.) We researched different companies and schools by pouring over *DANCE Magazine*, checking out books at the library, and watching videos and PBS specials. I became particularly obsessed with New York City Ballet because of the Hess girls' careers there. Loving NYCB means loving George Balanchine. I read everything I could find about him. He died the year I was born, and I decided that must mean something.

We had one studio at WTAMU, so class was always crowded. Rehearsals spilled out all over the building. We worked in atriums on tile floors and in empty university hall-ways with 1970s orange carpet. I loved how close we all were. Needing to work even at the barres to not crash into one another connected us as an ensemble. We were not the most talented college dance department, but we were known for always being well-spaced, coordinated, and clean in our work.

The best feature of our little Lone Star Ballet family studio was the hinged windows that opened enough to let us slip onto the sidewalk outside and lie on the sun-baked concrete for a rest between classes or safe place to roll our eyes when things got tense.

We toured and performed regularly. Our schedule looked like a menu, with shows in towns like Turkey and Mesquite, but we were happy to go. The freedom of being on the road with Lone Star Ballet fueled my drive to get to a big city company. Teachers at college dance festivals gave me encouragement, and I felt even more special knowing that those teachers didn't know just how young I was. We kept my age a secret. Small town applause reinforced my growing addiction to love from beyond the footlights. Our intense performance schedule gave me opportunity to become mentally flexible and a quick study. We rehearsed in parking lots, empty hotel bars, and on flatbeds of semi-trucks.

In the summers, I had to leave my sweet Lone Star Ballet home to attend the summer workshops where I had been accepted. Most professional ballet companies have a school attached, and these schools scout talent by hosting summer programs and running audition tours throughout the country to fill them. The first year I did auditions I didn't get accepted anywhere, but I was unpolished and only thirteen. I worked hard and had multiple acceptances the next year. I attended Ballet Austin and American Ballet Theater's satellite program at the University of Alabama. Each program was a four- to six week camp-like experience with all-day dance classes, workshops, seminars, and dorm life.

Telling Mr. Hess about my acceptance letters was always such a proud moment. He'd wag his finger, nod his head with an I-told-you-so air, smile, and say, "See. You work hard, and I tell you: things will happen." The next summer was spent at

Central Pennsylvania Youth Ballet. Anyone could attend that one, but in spite of the lack of auditions, their program provided some of the best training in the country. With every program I attended, I became more refined and more valuable to Mr. Hess and the Lone Star Ballet. Other dancers, like Aaron, began auditioning and attending workshops too.

* * *

I had a secret dancer boyfriend for six months of my senior year. Calvin was tall, handsome, straight, and liked me a lot. I liked him back. He moved to Amarillo the summer prior, and it didn't take us long to get together. We crushed hard for a while, and then on the way back from a Lone Star Ballet retreat he held my hand in the back of the fifteen-passenger van. I was not supposed to have a boyfriend at all, and I definitely was not supposed to have a non-Christian boyfriend. Calvin was more about Ayn Rand than Scripture.

I tried to get Calvin to church with me. I wanted him to mean it, but it would have been fine if he was faking. I wanted to be with him so badly, and I didn't want to have to lie to my parents. I loved that he would hold the small of my back through doorways, hug me, and tell me I was beautiful. He never used the word "pretty" but instead used "beautiful," "stunning," or dancey words like "graceful." I'd look toward him across the studio and see that he had been looking at me already. One night, in his dark living room after our friends intentionally left early, we sat buzzing on the couch like electromagnets. At the last possible moment before I needed to leave to make my curfew, we locked into my first kiss. I was won over and told him I would be his girl as long as no one officially knew.

Of course, the entire Lone Star Ballet knew. They gave me little bits of advice. They told me not to have sex (which I would never have done because I was scared abstinent by all the Crisis Pregnancy Center work my mom had done). They made sure Calvin was nice to me. They covered for us.

Calvin and I could talk for hours, but we almost never got the chance. It's hard to keep a secret boyfriend, and it's hard to talk while you're making out. Eventually, the stress of keeping him secret and the steady progression of our relationship started making me crazy. His parents were baffled as to why we "weren't dating," and it got harder to keep a lock on who knew we were together. I wanted to tell him I loved him, but instead I broke up with him. I was heartbroken, and so was he. He didn't talk to me at all for months. He hardly talked to anyone, and after a while he started being mean to me. He thought it was ridiculous that I wouldn't stand up for us. "But Calvin," I'd cry. "They will never let me leave if they can't trust me. And they will never be OK with me dating you. I have to be able to leave!"

I regretted all the kissing. He didn't want to just be my friend anymore, and I wanted his friendship so badly. When we danced, he went through the motions but no longer held me close. Every lift and touch had a coldness to it, and he'd avoid my eyes like a dog who's in trouble. Rehearsing for our final performance together was torture.

But during the show, I felt his hostility abate. Mid-*attitude promenade* he locked eyes with me like he used to do and smiled like I was beautiful to him again. On the rest of the turns and lifts he let the warm palm of his hand press into my body. After the curtain came down, all the seniors were overwhelmed with emotion. Calvin and I moved into the wings. He lifted me into a hug, and I didn't even check to make sure no one was watching. He kissed me one last time, and I didn't see him again after we both drove away from the parking lot.

* * *

My last year in Texas, they did stories about me on the local TV news. The back page of my scrapbook holds a newspaper article titled "Two Local Dancers Making Leaps" and has Aaron's headshot and mine. No wonder I was brave enough to strike out on my own, to shoot for the big leagues. I had the love of a community, a company I was proud of, a supportive family, and best friends.

My sixteen-year-old self is still in me. Heck, I think she's in charge most of the time. She's the one that wants to throw parties. She's the one who practices double *attitude* turns in the living room and checks to make sure I can still do the splits. She's the one who still loves Fountains of Wayne and is teaching the children to ask for Beck and Flaming Lips albums by name. She's the one who makes sure I'm wearing my lipstick.

NEW YORK

George Gershwin
"Rhapsody in Blue"

"'Just so youse'll know, this is NOT the train to Manhattan!" Mom and I looked at each other with eyebrows raised. We were the kind of Texans who could conceal our accents, and I felt a little smug that people from some place so cool as New York could carry such a heavy drawl. The cheapest tickets had us fly into ISLIP on Long Island, so we waited for the train to take us to Grand Central. I was vibrating with energy and could hardly believe any of this was actually happening.

My frugal family shelled out to bring me to New York City to audition for the School of American Ballet. I could have just gone to the cattle call in Dallas. That would have been much easier on everyone and on the finances, but the Hesses insisted that I needed to go right to the source. My audition was scheduled for noon the next day.

Riding the train, walking to the hotel, and venturing out to Lincoln Center, I felt like I was finally where I belonged. I was so delighted that reality lived up to my fantasies. I loved it!

There is a reason montages of new artists first experiencing New York are a thing. I felt a little anxious, but I had already learned that confidence was key. I threw my chest out, puffed open my little rib cage, lifted my chin, and hoped that the curls were blowing out behind me as I shot my heels forward on long-legged strides. "I have arrived, and for all you know, dear city, I've always been here! Fold me in!" If the opportunity had presented itself, I could've kissed my parents goodbye right then and there. Youthful ambition, courage, and joy—it was an unbeatable cocktail. Those dreams of seeing myself there, seeing myself in the mirrors of the New York City Ballet, superimposing my face on the ballet pictures in all my books filled me up and drove me ahead. No one had taught me visualization, but, boy, it was working its magic.

Auditions for the School of American Ballet Summer Intensive were held every Wednesday at noon. The pressure swelled. I thought of the money my parents were spending and of my sister, eleven years old, back in Texas, alone with my grandma. I thought of Mr. and Mrs. Hess. Without much lack of realism, I could imagine Mr. Hess saying to all the college dancers, "You know Jessica is in New York City. You all should have goals like that." I could see him staring up into the corners of the studio and pulling out the comb as he pictured me there at Lincoln Center. Mrs. Hess would use me to make other girls feel bad about themselves. "You think Jessica's going to bend over and pant like that at City Ballet?! She better not! You people are lazy."

The ballet world was small, and I'd occupied enough hours and corners in it to know that SAB was the place for rich girls and young little phenoms. I was not rich and, already sixteen, old to be just arriving. This was a place for the special, and I was pretty regular as ballet hopefuls went. I labored under no delusions. The only thing phenomenal about me was my courage, lack of anxiety, and guilelessness, but I didn't know that then. Back then I just had that "Why shouldn't good things happen to me?" kind of attitude that always helps a girl out.

Looking back twenty years, I see a skinny, smiling, curly-headed circus girl who escaped the tent. The pressures filled a giant orb beneath my dancing, slippered feet. If I could just manage it all a bit longer, then I'd get out of Texas and be on to my grand adventure. I had to keep the boyfriend a secret, not talk back, try not to argue, and keep Mrs. Hess from crushing me. Somehow, pure joy and hope suspended me so I could roll and ride that big ball, just barely maintaining control and guiding it through my routine. I could see the anxiety on other people's faces, my mom's in particular, but I laughed it off from high on my perch.

Mom and Dad flanked me and my unwieldy ball of hopes and dreams, along for the ride and trying to guide it, knowing that if this bubble ever burst, I would be absolutely shocked by the crash. I had no idea how precarious my ambitions made me. They let me do it though. My dad wanted me to find what he had not. He was a musician, one who could have found some fame if he'd been given parental support and taken his industry friends up on their offers. My mom could see how much I loved it all.

We told the security guard I had an audition at the School of American Ballet. The moment felt wildly special to me, and dismissively mundane to him. Juilliard, SAB, the New York City Ballet, and the dorms for each are all in one tall tower of Lincoln Center. Ten years ago I could have still told you what organization or branch was held on every floor. My earliest memory of the School of American Ballet is January, gray and white, outside and in. The carpet was a cement shade not too different than the marley floors inside. The studios were the most beautiful I had ever seen, with high windows welcoming light onto the ground. Shiny, black grand pianos occupied a corner of every room. The barres were pine.

Another girl was there to audition too, and I was instantly

intimidated. First, she was named "Thalia." Contrasted with my number one name of the '80s, that name was surely bound for stardom (like "Alexia"). She wore a leotard with a mock-turtleneck top made of a shimmering, red lycra. There was a stripe of contrasting color just under where breasts would be which highlighted her thin, ribby torso just right. On the back, a stretchy, mesh fabric with no slouches or draping spread across her back from the nape of her neck to beneath the sharp, visible shoulder blades. I just had on a black camisole leotard in regular stretch cotton with a gather on the neckline, probably made by me with a safety pin. I felt inadequate and knew that I could definitely not find a leotard like Thalia's in the Discount Dance Supply catalog. To top her off, she had an elaborate French twist in her perfect, natural, dark red hair. I felt like a mouse, a country mouse, next to her.

I was afraid of her until she opened her mouth. "I'm so nervous," she said, and I could hear in her wavering tone that she really was. "Me too," I said with a strong, calm voice, and I wasn't lying but was definitely being nice. That's when I saw that she balled and un-balled her fists, that there was already sweat on her breast bone, that her mother hovered within sight (while I had banished mine to stay far away). I remember Thalia so well because she was prototypical of the young dancers I'd get to know over the next few years. Her leotard was custom-made, and I would never have one that nice. My hair wasn't thick enough to make a twist like hers. My mother would never have any sway in whether my dance career lived or died. But I would never, ever be as wracked with terror as Thalia was. There was a level of anxiety in these girls that reminded me of those fancy, tiny dogs that are shaking no matter what. I was a Golden Retriever among them.

Suki Schorer, a small, buzzing woman, came briskly around the corner hips first. "OK, girls." She shot her gaze and chin up and around when she spoke like Cheri Oteri in a 1990s SNL skit. I knew who she was. She was in my books back home. I knew she was an important teacher at the school.

"OK, girls. Come into the studio, and we'll begin with testing your legs."

Go right ahead, I thought. *Test my legs.* I have been heard bragging to my children about being one of the most flexible people in the country when I was a ballet dancer. True? Who can say? I was no Cirque du Soleil contortionist actor, but I had the most flexible hips of anyone I'd actually met. At any summer program I'd been to, of anyone I'd seen on *Great Performances*, I had the highest side extensions and frequently was acknowledged for it. As Suki Schorer asked for my leg and I *battement*'ed it gracefully up into her hands, I was downright filled with glee. She could push that leg anywhere she wanted and back again. My *a la seconde* extension could pass the 180-degree mark and then some. I could make my right ankle pass behind my head and come out past my left ear. She was pleased, and this was a very good note on which to begin. Thalia was obviously disturbed. *If only she knew*, I thought. *That's as good as I get.*

We danced through a truncated class, and I did fine. I used everything I'd ever learned. I remember being distressed about the turns. I generally had trouble getting my spindly body organized for pirouettes and had told Mrs. Hess before I left that I just hoped there wouldn't be a lot of turning. "I always worry about the pirouettes," I said.

"Why?" she scoffed at me. "You don't have any problem with pirouettes."

She might as well have said, "These are not the droids you are looking for." The effect was the same! Her Jedi mind trick didn't make me an instant turning success, but it sure did a lot to remove anxiety from the equation. So, in that side studio at the School of American Ballet, when it really, really mattered, I didn't have any problem with pirouettes. I remember landing solid, clean doubles with good suspension at the end, and in that context, that was all I needed. Suki didn't ask for my other nemesis, *entrechat six* (jump up and beat your legs so that you change which foot is in front 3 times before you land). All the *petite allegro* was fine and fun like it should be, and I could jump quite high in the *grand allegro*.

Walking out, I thought, *That wasn't so bad! I actually danced OK!* No falls. No sloppy turns. And my Gumby legs had definitely been noticed. All in a day's work for a little ballet hopeful on her first trip to Mecca. I wished Thalia *merde* and breezed out to my parents with a smile on my face.

* * *

There was one thing I asked my dad not to do. As a firstborn child, I always identified more with adults than kids, so my parents didn't embarrass me. Kids embarrassed me. But that afternoon I said, "Please, Dad. Please remember that I've never, ever asked you for anything like this ever. Please don't do that thing where you run into the door jamb, dishevel your glasses, and look stunned. PLEASE."

My request indicated nervousness, the fact that New York City did actually make me feel like a kid. He assured me he wouldn't, but the impish look on his face drove me crazy and said to me, "Chill out, chick." Exiting the fancy building, he shot his eyes back over his shoulder at me as he glided past the security guard and the door frame without incident. Giddy relief rippled through me as we set out toward Broadway.

The difficult business behind us, we lived it up for the rest of the trip. Across from the ballet, a restaurant named Josephina served me veal meatballs over angel hair. The restaurant was mediocre, actually, but when that waiter came over with a little gold tray and scraper to clean up crumbs between our basket of bread and the arrival of our main courses, this little Amarillo baby about lost it.

Dad had come home from work a few weeks earlier and

said, "Hey! Why don't you find us some hot tickets for after your audition? We can do whatever you want!" Oh, how I loved it when he was like that! I didn't have to ponder, of course. I had a calendar of New York City Ballet programming in my school desk. *Fancy Free*, Balanchine's version of sailors on leave for one perfect day in Manhattan, was playing that Wednesday night. 'Nuff said.

Before the show, we paused next to sculptures in the lobby of New York State Theater for photos and wondered whether they were important. Not that I cared. The picture was to be of me looking young and pretty in a sparkly black dress. I loved every moment of the performance, and by the time we flew back to Texas the next day, I was sure my feet could never touch the ground again.

ACCEPTANCE

Love me love me
Pretend that you love me...

The Cardigans
"Lovefool" from *First Band on the Moon*

I remember seeing my friend Casey's face especially. A vocal performance major, his smile could warm a whole room, and his voice was big and beautiful. "Did you hear?" I said to him. "Did you hear my news?"

"Yes!" Casey said. "I'm so proud of you. Our little ballerina got a scholarship to TCU!"

"NO! Not that," I said. "I got into SAB!"

For me, the half tuition academic scholarship and first alternate position for the ballet scholarship at Texas Christian University felt more like threats. I was proud to have earned them, but I was afraid that the security and the financial help of going to TCU would keep my parents from letting me do what I really wanted: go to New York and become a dancer.

I was accustomed to waiting for "the letter" to arrive. I knew that big, fat envelopes were good and that skinny, standard-sized letters were bad. The first word would be "Thank you" if you did not get in and "Congratulations" if you did. I would skip out to the mailbox everyday after the mailman rounded out of the cul-de-sac. The metal mailbox gave that satisfying resistance when you pulled the door down. Getting it open was an accomplishment, and whenever I was waiting on a letter, it was like opening a present. Even when there were rejections to be read, I was still glad to have the waiting period complete.

I had finally opened the mailbox to see an acceptance packet to the School of American Ballet's Summer Program. I still consider it one of the top ten happiest days of my life. (It would be on an even shorter list, but I have four children!) That packet was the validation I needed, and it came at exactly the right time. I needed all the evidence I could gather to convince my family that pursuing a career in dance was reasonable.

I knew college would be a cakewalk for me. I knew I could be successful, and all my college acceptance letters and scholarship offers seemed proof. "See?" I told my parents. "That will always be there. I can always go to college if I need to, but if I don't try as hard as I can to be a dancer, I will wonder about it my whole life. I have to know if I can do it. And if I don't go for it now, I'll never be able to again."

I was right. At that time, dancers were entering ballet companies around the age of eighteen. I knew that there were girls my age who had already been training full-time at prestigious ballet schools like School of American Ballet, Pacific Northwest Ballet, and San Francisco Ballet. Kids went to boarding schools for the arts like Interlochen or North Carolina School of the Arts. I considered myself behind already. I could hold my own against the full-time kids, but they were more refined; and they definitely knew more about how everything worked. I was just an excited kid from Amarillo, Texas, with rubber joints, optimism, and deep, satisfying happiness while in a studio. I had a love for art and believed everything I heard about the power and importance of art in the world. I wanted in. I wanted it bad, and this SAB acceptance was my toe in the door.

In ballet, we don't mess around with self-esteem. You are either accepted or rejected.

* * *

The plan was vague, but for me it began with flying off to New York City. With naive fearlessness, I was certain it would all work out for me. I'd deferred my entrance at Fordham University, the school closest to School of American Ballet. Maybe that could work somehow. Maybe I would make the right friends and figure out how to rent a tiny apartment somewhere in the city. I didn't know how, but I was planning to do everything I could to keep myself in Manhattan.

The Spring leading up to my New York summer, I put myself in a little self-inflicted boot camp. I wore pointe shoes all the time, no matter how badly my feet hurt. Normally, we wouldn't wear them for a whole class. No one ever made us, but I knew that I would have to do that at SAB. I loved wearing pointe shoes, but unbeknownst to me at the time, my shoes did not fit well for my feet. There was no place to go get fitted. I had to take my chances and order based on catalog descriptions. The shoes didn't fit my bones correctly, so they rubbed in all the wrong places. By the halfway point in most classes, my feet would be aching, sometimes bleeding. But I never took them off and wore the red badge of toughness on the outside of my shoes once the blood soaked through.

There were other tortures. Aaron and I would give each other ideas for freakish stretches and conditioning exercises. In addition to my four hours of class and four hours of rehearsals every day, I would stretch my feet by sliding between the *barre* and the wall, driving the ball of my foot into the floor, pressing my butt and heel against the wall, and using my arms to support my attempt to straighten the leg all the way. I would lie on my bedroom floor at night and do the splits every which way with one leg on my bed and one on a chair, my hips hanging down as low as I could stand in the middle. After everyone was asleep, I'd be in there doing bridges and back bends. My goal was to be able to do a backbend and then continue bending backward, come down to my forearms on the floor, and look back toward my butt and feet upside down. Then there were squats, inner thigh squeezes, and crunches. I would put a blanket at the base of the door to block light from shining out from my room.

I learned the concept of "second wind" when I told my dad about passing one hundred crunches and then strangely feeling a wave of fresh energy and continuing on to two hundred.

He said, "Sounds like you found your second wind! When did you do that?"

"Oh around eleven last night."

All that time I was worried that I might not be working hard enough.

DEVIL'S SLIDE

We live in cities that you'll never see on screen.

Lorde
"Team" from *Pure Heroine*

When my dad was a kid, his mom and her friends would take turns picking up their middle schoolers on Friday afternoons to drive them down to the canyon. These women would drive them there and leave them alone until Sunday. I'm pretty sure they'd bring beef jerky, a pocket knife, a canteen, and some fire-crackers. With that long leash, my parents' generation came up with great canyon stories, and my friends and I just waited until we could go off and have our own adventures. We collected legends and challenges and swapped them back and forth.

I first heard about "Devil's Slide" in the back of some mom's car on a field trip. As the elements break down the walls of the canyon, they cascade into the undulating, half-cone, slippery, lovely Spanish Skirts. They are red, yellow, white, purple, even a greenish color. You cannot really climb up the skirts because the dirt gives way easily and makes you slide backwards into pointy rocks or cacti at the bottom. BUT, legend had it that there was one spot where, if you did it right, you could hike to the top of the skirt and slide down without meeting any pokey end. People would supposedly drag up pieces of cardboard and slide down. It was Texan sledding.

I thought that sounded pretty amazing and like something I definitely needed to do as soon as I was allowed to go to the canyon without adults. Every time I rode to the floor of the canyon and wound through the state park loop, I'd look for Devil's Slide based on the spot pointed out to me on that field trip in third grade years ago.

When I was sixteen, a group of Lone Star Ballet dancers headed to the canyon one June with every intention of finding and riding Devil's Slide. I was in heaven: childhood dream come true, plus Aaron was there. When Calvin got angry with me, I slipped back into my affection for Aaron. We found the spot pretty easily, or at least we found a huge Spanish skirt that looked like maybe we could careen down without being smashed at the end. However, adventure was a much higher priority than were safety or planning.

After we made it to the top by hiking up the side of the slide we quickly realized, "This is freaking steep and maybe this isn't an awesome idea." Suddenly, we heard a scrabbling, scraping noise and saw that Angus, the guy in front, was sliding down on his feet in a standing position. He screamed a bit and then managed to crouch down and slide all the way down in a squat. As he yelled back to us that he was OK, the next guy started to slip and went down. Then the next. As I watched them, I remember thinking, *I hope I'm not about to ruin my life. I've got scholarships in New York City, and I need to get out of Texas.* But, one after another, the rest of my friends committed and went sliding down this crease in the skirt. I had hopes of controlling my descent somewhat and creeped to the point of no return.

I was wearing Keds and seriously questioned my choice. They aren't known for their traction, and as I started to slide into the area with the softened dirt, my shoes filled up on the sides. Within a couple seconds, I recognized that I would have *zero* control of my descent, and I quickly sat down into a full fetal-position-like squat and began flying down the hill. It was thrillingly fun and completely terrifying. The dirt stream I was in avoided the few boulders that littered the edges of the skirt, and I kept my hands up to avoid the scrubby cacti and other barbed plants. Around the third second of my Devil's Slide, my body played a diabolical trick. I noticed the warm spread of urine. I tried to shut it down, but there was no way.

I full-on peed the entire rest of the way down. Sadly, this meant that I had hardly any attention span or joy related to my surviving and finally achieving a trip down Devil's Slide because now I was wearing it all over my backside. Don't worry: my pants were white. They were my favorite pants, the kind that only a sixteen-year-old ballet dancer could really pull off. Of course, I had worn my favorite outfit for my very grown-up day in the canyon with my cool college friends and my (gay) not-boyfriend. I had no hope that this would be something I could cover up.

Having lived through our stupidity, everyone was high-fiving, laughing, just generally rejoicing that no one was injured, and through it all I just kept the back of my body facing out of the circle at all times. When I had the chance as we walked back toward the cars, I confided to the one other girl in the group: "Ummm, I peed my pants on the way down. I was terrified and tried to stop the peeing, but there was just no way." Her next words were a balm to my soul.

"So did I."

Thank you, God, I thought. And I was sort of saying thank you for letting me go down Devil's Slide, but mostly I was just grateful that my cool college friend had also peed her pants. We both sported wet, muddy, red circles on our butts for the hike of shame down to the water crossing where we went in the creek in our clothes to rinse out our pants. I was slated to ride home with Aaron, the best part of the day that I was looking forward to. I was so enamored with him, but I did have a sense that there was something keeping us apart. As I opened his passenger door to get in. He said, "Do you think you could sit on this towel?"

I was mortified to ride in Aaron's Volvo on a towel, but we were all so close that I felt OK. In a few weeks, I'd be leaving the comfort and safety of the Lone Star Ballet. I wouldn't be the star anymore. I'd have to make new friends. And I'd better not pee my pants.

BICOASTAL SUMMER

You realize the sun doesn't go down
It's just an illusion caused by the world spinning round

The Flaming Lips
"Do You Realize" from *Yoshimi Battles the Pink Robots*

The School of American Ballet was all I had dreamed it would be. The classes were difficult for me. Balanchine technique is very specific, and while Mr. Hess generally taught in that style, there were many specificities, hand positions, use of *plié*, etc., that were new and awkward to learn. I loved it though. My poor little feet had a hard time. The pointe shoes I had used all spring led to my developing soft corns between my baby and ring toes. The joint rubbed against the bone of the neighboring toe and ate away the tissue in between creating painful abscesses on both feet. One turned to cellulitis, and I had to spend a while on antibiotics and a couple days sitting out of class. After that, Susan Pilarre taught me how to cut a hole in the side of my pointe shoe so that the injured toe had more space to heal.

Then I took a walk to the Freed of London store and was properly fit for pointe shoes for the first time in my life. The store is not fancy, but I brimmed over with admiration. One wall had a mirror and barre, and the rest were lined with boxes and boxes of pointe shoes. There were shoes there that had been specially designed for individual dancers but were no longer wanted. I was fit in shoes that had been rejected by a soloist in Seattle. Dancing on pointe became much less painful, and I used only a folded paper towel for padding and found the shoes much more comfortable. I learned about the maker stamps, symbols pressed into the leather with which the cobblers signed their work. From then on I wore clubs, anchors, and sometimes crowns in a size 5X.

The social time was incredible. I was a friendly, funny girl who made friends easily. I could usually identify a group I wanted to join and have it done in a couple of days. To have some of the cost knocked off my room and board, I worked as a resident advisor, like a camp counselor for the younger kids in the dorm. As a result, I chaperoned field trips to all manner of NYC tourist activities and amazing arts events like *Annie Get Your Gun* on Broadway starring Bernadette Peters, *The Lion King,* the New York Philharmonic, American Ballet Theater, and a quick road trip to Sarasota, the New York City Ballet's summer residence. It was a glamorous heaven! Summer was hot and wonderful. I sat on the top level of a double-decker tour bus feeling like a million bucks. Every Wednesday night there were free social dances and lessons on the Lincoln Center Plaza. I learned to swing dance with some stranger as I missed Calvin and Aaron.

My friends and I celebrated my seventeenth birthday at the Hard Rock Cafe. We were so broke that we just drank sodas and ate fries. (Well, the boys and I ate fries while the other girls starved themselves and wondered whether the soda was actually diet.) They brought me a plate of whip cream with a Hard Rock flag and a candle in it.

The five-week Summer Intensive at SAB was coming to a close, and I needed something to happen. I had turned down my dean's scholarship at Texas Christian University and my acceptance at NYU. Fordham was still an option. I had been accepted and even received some scholarship money. Fordham's campus is right by Lincoln Center where the School of American Ballet is. I was hoping for them to either accept me and let me stay in the housing there or for them to at least let me in the school. I needed to find a way to be in a full-time professional training program. I even sucked it up to introduce myself to Peter Boal after he taught my class. "You signed my ballet shoe when I was little at Lone Star Ballet. Alexia Hess is from my studio!"

"Yes, we were there with Zippora," he said.

"Right," I said. I think I spent my whole little life just wishing for connection to the big leagues.

Seventeen is old. At New York City Ballet, at least at that time, very young dancers were being made apprentices in the company at fifteen or sixteen years old. And honestly, I wasn't good enough. I was so, so green. I just hadn't had the kind of training I needed yet. That was the problem! I was a ball of raw material, desperately longing for training, but not polished enough to get in at SAB, not at the ripe old age of seventeen and a height of 5' 8". I barely remember the conversation that changed the course of my life. It took so much guts to ask if I could stay, to just ask them to please think about it. My happy-go-lucky, Texas-sized chutzpah served me well. Looking back, I know I was not the right candidate, but I wanted to dance and be in the city. It made me brave enough to ask anyway.

"Well, I'm not sure it would work for you to be here." Or something like that. I do remember telling my parents that Suki, the SAB teacher with curls, said, "Peter [Martens] is just taking shorter dancers these days." I'm sure she did give me that impression, but now I can't remember the sound of her voice exactly or what she said. I do know that the idea of going to Seattle came from her on that day, and she did say she would be willing to call and recommend me to the Pacific Northwest Ballet School (PNBS).

I planned and scheduled the audition trip to Seattle from my dorm room. I headed home to Texas by myself with a lot of excitement and hope even though everything was still so very uncertain. I had made several sweet friends from PNBS during my weeks at Lincoln Center, and one, Caitlin, promised that her family would love to help me. Another told me that his family rented their attic to exchange students. Kids at camp still exchanged addresses for writing letters, and I wrote Caitlin asking her to call me and give me more confirmation that they could actually let me stay with them when I arrived to audition.

* * *

I flew to Seattle all by myself. Having practiced in New York City and being way too big for my britches, it didn't scare me at all to get a taxi alone from the airport to uptown Seattle where Pacific Northwest Ballet is located on the same grounds as the Space Needle. My mom and dad had planned it all out for me, and I followed their directions exactly. I had never been to Seattle. My main impression of the city was from a Rice Krispies commercial that played Saturday mornings when I was a kid. I expected Grunge culture, deciduous trees, and skate boarders.

In the cab, I observed conifers dominating the landscape and was a bit disappointed. I didn't yet know that Washington is the Evergreen State. I eagerly waited to see whether another expectation would be met or changed. An old summer room-mate lived in Tacoma, Washington. She told me how the drive into Seattle provided a magical moment when the Seattle skyline suddenly rose into view. Her name was Jamie, and all she wanted was to dance at PNBS. I wondered if I would see her as I first picked out the Space Needle on the horizon. It was August, so the weather was spectacular.

I was dropped off at the ballet school, at 301 Mercer Street, a few hours before my audition class was to be held. When I was fourteen, the son of the original directors of PNB had come to Amarillo to guest as the Sugar Plum Cavalier for our Nutcracker. Mr. or Mrs. Hess had prompted me to ask him whether he could help me get into PNBS, or something like that. He wrote the address for me and told me to send a request for information about their Summer Course. I knew even then that it was his nice way of brushing me off. But there I was on Mercer Street. I recognized the front steps from the brochures I'd received.

A woman greeted me from the other side of the front desk and sent me to kill some time at the grocery store up the road. When I walked in, I was instantly in love. Larry's was a beautiful store with a huge deli. I grabbed a carton of potato salad and a bottle of Dr. Pepper. I sat for the first time in the minty green booths and ate that delicious, perfect potato salad. I can still taste the balance of the onion with the sweetness of pickle relish and the soft, salty red potatoes set off by crunchy celery. I should have been terrified, but I just wasn't. I have no memories of fear or anxiety from that day, only an intense excitement. Everything was working out so exactly as planned!

I headed back to the studios after my snack and took my time getting ready. I wore a black leotard. I did my hair in an elaborate bun. As always, I got my lipstick on perfectly and wore dangly earrings. The dressing room was large, clean, and well-designed. The whole school was nice! PNB's interior colors are mostly mauves and tans, and it all felt very well-loved and prided. The studios were light, spacious, and airy. They were such inspirational places to dance.

There was one other girl, Jennifer, there to audition for the year-round program. I was intimidated because she was from North Carolina School of the Arts. The teacher who would evaluate us had that air of superiority that all good auditioners should have, but she was not nearly as intimidating as the SAB teachers. Class went very well. I hit my turns and held a shockingly good, long balance in the pointe combination. I felt maybe I would fool them that I was better than I really was! Of course, my legs could always go the highest, so I knew that would help me too.

After the class, I waited to be called into the conference room. Back then, there were seven levels in the school. I only expected to be considered for Level VII, though I knew there was also a Professional Division (like a level VIII) for girls and boys like me who were ready for year-round, intensive training. The PD's often would perform with the company and had classes multiple times a day. I didn't think I would be considered for that since I had never attended even a Summer Course at PNB. At thirteen, I had auditioned for them and felt out of control and clueless, and I didn't get in. Word on the street was that PNB had a long memory and wouldn't take people that had been rejected before. So I really didn't know what to expect.

"Well, we can offer you a place in the Professional Division."

"What?!" I answered. "As a PD? Are you sure?"

"Yes. Should we change our minds?"

"NO! That's wonderful! I'm just surprised!"

I really wish I had been privy to the conversation in the office that must have taken place after my little self had said all that. Years later, I heard lots of conversations about lots of girls, but I'm pretty certain no one else reacted quite like I did that day. It was pure, embarrassing joy. I didn't yet know any better than to be honest and myself.

I was over the moon when I called my parents to tell them. As Caitlin's dad drove me to their house, I poured over Seattle with hungry eyes. I would live here! I was going to the Pacific Northwest Ballet School! I hadn't even thought of Seattle at all since I had been rejected for that Summer Course. I just believed the rumors that they wouldn't ever let me in, but here I was! A PD! My longest, best-known dream, to become a professional dancer, was coming true.

Right there in Mr. Cooney's car, a new dream to live in Seattle bloomed before my eyes. He played tour guide and showed me everything of interest, including Mount Rainier. I didn't even know that Mt. Rainier existed until he pointed at it through the car window across Lake Washington as we traversed the 520 floating bridge. I remember him saying, "Mt. Fuji-like in appearance," and I was in love. I had never, ever seen or imagined anything like it. Lakes, mountains, trees, bridges, Space Needle, sparkling downtown skyscrapers. The Pacific Northwest is like a Vegas buffet. I kept thinking, *Can I really have all of this at once?*

INTERMEZZO

ON STAGE

In an opera house or other theater, there are two kinds of air. One body of air is heated by the stage lighting and filled with the hearty exhales of dancers warming up their bodies. This is the air behind the curtain, and it smells like old paint and clean sweat. The audience breathes the air of the house. It is cool, too cool usually. It smells like carpet and playbills fresh from the printer. It carries bits and pieces of melody as oboists or trumpeters practice their solos.

The stage manager calls, "Places!" and the dancers become still. The house lights dim, and the audience goes quiet. Everyone takes a big draw of their own air through their noses. The conductor taps the podium, and the orchestra begins to play. But it hasn't happened quite yet. The heavy, velvet meridian still holds the two bodies of air apart from each other. The audience and dancers wait for each other for just a few more moments.

I remember noticing the different air as a young girl. Suzanne Farrell describes it as well in her autobiography, *Holding on to the Air*. Whenever on stage, I always brought my awareness to the air before, during, and after the curtain went up. I made note of the breezes and swirls fluttering my tulle costumes and was sure to enjoy it, to tell myself, "It's happening now." Feeling the audience air reminded me of their presence in the blackness. Audiences don't really get a sense of how stage air feels. Only the performer is able to enjoy that part of the sensory experience. Like the little girl mesmerized by floating dust in a school gym, I let myself wonder and absorb as much as I could. On stage I experienced deep gratitude and contentment.

* * *

To prepare for a ballet performance, I first walk to the stage door. I show my badge to Linny the cheerful attendant and head for the stairs. My makeup is waiting for me where I left it in my fourth floor dressing room. Hierarchy at the theater works backwards from the corporate world. Primas are on stage level, and people like me are in the rafters.

I toss down my bag, then strip and fold up my street clothes. If there's a warm-up class, I put on a leotard and black tights or sweatpants and run down to the stage to find a place to stand. I go through the movements called out by the ballet mistress and pay way too much attention to whether or not anyone is watching me. Afterward, we all clap and head back to the stairs.

I get into my pink tights and trunks and slide into a zip-up sweatshirt or button-up cardigan. If it's too hot from all the lit mirrors, I may just wear an old t-shirt with a very wide neck. I need to be able to get out of the dressing clothes without catching my hair or smearing my makeup.

I slick my hair taught using cheap gel and that precious Aquanet before I start my face. I slather on foundation and then face powder. I use a bright blush to highlight my cheekbones. The eyebrows are shaped and darkened, and then I fuss with the glue and false eyelashes. If I don't stab my tear duct, it's a good day. I cover my whole eyelid in a shimmering white. A darker shadow goes in the crease, and then I pick a pretty, bright color to tap on the outer corners and along my lashline. I line my eyes in black, and sprinkle however much microscopic glitter that I think I can get away with. Bright lipstick goes on smooth and easy.

I put on my pointe shoes.

The music for the show is piped into the dressing room along with the stage manager's calls. When the auditory cues tell me it's time, I head toward the dressers, the quiet women doing crossword puzzles and knitting. I tell them my last name, and they grab my costume. I'm not supposed to put it on without them. My attendant apologizes for her cold hands as she reaches down to my tailbone to start pulling the bodice tight around me. Every costume has rows and rows of hooks and eyes. The dressers have learned quickly which row is mine, and they wrap me up like a present. I shift and pull at the costume to make sure it's right.

Heading back down the stairs, I shake my head around to make sure the headpiece is secure. We quiet our chatter as we approach the rosin box on the side stage. I untie my shoe and slip off the back of it, so I can rub my heel in the rosin. I may rosin my shoes as well; it depends. I tie them back up and make sure the ends are tucked in tightly before I hairspray them one last time.

I go to my wing and make eye contact with my opposite. Maybe we mime or dance for each other a bit if no one else is watching. Then I bring my awareness to the air and tune into the music.

Five, six, seven, and....

PART II

THE WAY THINGS WORKED

I had years to gradually learn how ballet advancement works. I've distilled it all into an infographic on the next page. Time moves from top to bottom. Every arrow represents a possible path for a dancer from one tier to another. The number of shapes is proportional for the most part. For example, there are many more regional ballet companies (Ballet Idaho, Cincinnati Ballet) than major ballet companies (New York City Ballet, Pacific Northwest Ballet) and MANY more college dance departments than ballet training schools (though not all dance departments are created equal! And they don't all have great ballet.).

"Arts Schools" refers to places like North Carolina School of the Arts, Interlochen, La Guardia, etc. Notice that many arrows go into auditions but few come out! When I was dancing, most major ballet schools only accepted around 10 to 15 percent of those who auditioned for Summer Course.

I did not include international companies and possibilities in this flowchart, but ballet thrives around the world.

* * *

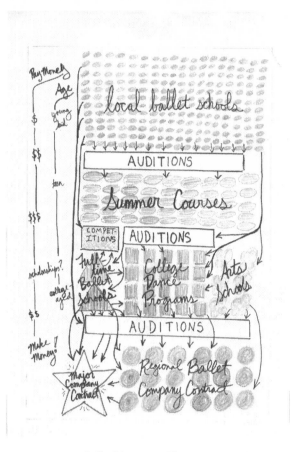

Ballet Advacement Circa 2001

Another option ballet students sometimes choose is to make a jump to other forms of dance and theater like modern or musical theater.

Teaching or choreography are also options, but unless someone had some semblance of a career in ballet, she is very unlikely to find a job teaching in a major school, or even a smaller school. When she does get a teaching job, she's likely to start with very young children.

From my observation, teaching and choreography have their own hierarchies and flowcharts.

THE MOVE

My dreams kept on growing 'til I couldn't stay.
A seed on the wind, I twirled far away.
Planted and rooted, you only could watch,
looking back up across all those big city blocks
at all of the places that held me inside.
Oh, that season is over, but nobody died.

Jessica Ribera
"When in Rome"

For three days the Meador family drove across the western United States. We had lunch in Denver the first day and then slept in Wyoming. I left my phone charger in Boise the next day, and that caused a lot of stress in Seattle on day three. I had always wanted to leave, but now that it was happening, I wavered a bit. It manifested not in tears or words of doubt but in scatter-brained forgetfulness and a lack of patience for my parents' stress.

Dad was in his element: navigating, managing, double-checking, but he was antsy and short with me. I can only imagine how they felt. The faith required to drive your seventeen-year-old daughter eighteen hundred miles away and leave her in a foreign place, as we like to say, "would kill a normal man." Mom did lots of managing and planning, but she kept quiet, a little pensive. She was only thirty-nine years old, and I was already leaving.

I kept thinking, *I'm the one moving. I'm the one about to be alone!* I resented the perceived requirement that I be perfectly reassuring, thankful, and respectful at all times. Granted, I should have been thankful and respectful. And I was! But I did not think I could be nervous or sensitive. If I acted out, I worried it would make my parents more apprehensive. I remember telling myself, "I just have to hang on. I have to watch my mouth and be good for the next two days, and then I can relax. I'll get all this figured out once they leave." Just as when I went to audition for PNBS, my parents had made every plan for us. I couldn't believe they were letting me go, and I didn't want to screw it up! That weekend fit the pattern of my life: me trying to be a grown-up, unable to escape the fact that I really was a child.

The first Sunday in Seattle was a great example. We had scouted a potential church home by searching the internet and drove to it avoiding all freeways because my parents didn't want me driving on them. Once inside, Mom and Dad marched me up to the head pastor and (in a speech that has become Green Lake Presbyterian Church legend) said, "This is our daughter Jessica. She's seventeen and here to dance with the Pacific Northwest Ballet. Please take care of her!" I found it embarrassing and reassuring at the same time. I wanted independence, but care sounded good too.

We had arranged for me to live in the spare bedroom of my friend's house. Everything had clicked into place. When my family left, I fell back onto the giant waterbed in my oddly-shaped room and exhaled. I had one day, Labor Day, to rest before I started swimming with the big fish.

FINDING MY SPOT

Been talking 'bout the way things change
And my family lives in a different state
And if you don't know what to make of this
Then we will not relate

The Head and the Heart
"Rivers and Roads" from *The Head and the Heart*

I took my freeway-free route to the ballet, parked in the big garage, and anxiously headed inside. For the first time since I showed up at the Hess School of Dance, I felt intimidated. I was so glad to see Jenny from my audition in the dressing room, and I was ready to be her best friend if she'd let me. Being in the PD locker section was overwhelming. There were obviously rules and norms that I knew nothing about. Only four of us were coming in brand-new that fall; the rest of the girls (and all the boys) had just completed the Summer Course, and one half of the class was on a second year of the Professional Division program.

Butterflies of many names danced in my tummy: fear, happiness, loneliness, embarrassment, excitement. My mind was all over the place, but one thought loomed largest: where will I stand?

The question had two meanings. 1) Which spot at the *barre* should I choose? And, 2) How on earth will I compare to these other girls? I wondered whether I would be the greenest and an embarrassment. The latter concern would be ever-present my entire first year at PNBS. Truthfully, in some ways I was the worst dancer there. I also was the youngest by a year, except for Carla and Drew. Drew Jacoby was sixteen years old, six-feet-tall, and destined for greatness. Even the first day, I knew it would be best not to compare myself to her.

The question of spot at the barre, however, was of immediate concern and primary importance. Ballet is hierarchical and comparative by its very design and nature, and that sense trickles down to the very youngest students. Having been the biggest fish in my Lone Star Ballet pond, I never had to concern myself with deference my last few years there. I did what I wanted (and was mostly Elise-inspired kind), and everyone let me have my way. At Summer Courses, everyone was new together, so no one had to worry about offending a veteran. PNB was a new scene for me, and I was painfully aware of my status as an outsider.

Coming into the studio, I took a deep breath and looked around. With relaxed faces and attitudes, the second-years were already getting settled and even pointed out places to stand for the incoming dancers they knew from Summer Course. But no one knew me. I was crushed to see Jenny chatting and laughing with friends she knew from the other ballet schools she'd attended. I shook it off and pictured Alexia Hess. What would she have done? She would have calmed down and picked a place! So I did and dropped to the floor to start stretching.

Then a steely-faced, stressed out, tall dancer with legs for days, charged into the room with her arms full of stuff. "Umm-mm," she said with more attitude than one person should even be able to contain. She marched from the door to right where I was and said with plentiful disgust, "You are in my spot." Her eye roll displayed the reason grown-ups say, "Your face is gonna stick that way."

"Oh, sorry," I said. "But it's the first day, right?" (I pep-talked myself in my head: *Be Alexia! Be Alexia!*) "It's probably OK for there to be some new spots, yeah?"

"Uch! So you aren't going to move?" (Eyes rolling! Mouth hanging open!)

"Well, I can scooch a bit, but we're pretty full here now." Around the room I could see a few downcast faces smile a bit. It had gotten quiet. She glared at me and bit her teeth tight together behind her pursed lips for a full couple seconds before she spun around and threw her arms up in the air, pointe shoe ribbons flying high. "Well, I can see I won't be getting along with anyone here this year!" She marched to another corner of the room and threw her stuff on the floor. Everyone around the room made faces and sneakily chuckled, rolling their eyes and shaking their heads at each other.

The reactions from everyone else indicated to me that this girl was probably a wild card and that I'd done the right thing by standing my ground. When the teacher came in and class began, I felt strengthened and encouraged by that little scene with the big city ballet student. *Here we go*, I thought to myself. *I think I'm going to be alright.*

* * *

By the end of the week I had figured out the social structures, though not my own place in it all. There were the tall, silly-but-mature, second-year girls who seemed to have no cares in the world even though they would all be vying for contracts with ballet companies by the end of the year.

There were the SAB kids. I hadn't met any of them because while I was in New York, they were doing the Summer in Seattle.

Acquaintances of mine from SAB Summer did attend PNBS year-round, like Caitlin who had hosted me for my audition, but they were well-established in their friend groups. They were perfectly nice to me, some of the nicest people in the school, actually, but I didn't feel like I fit with them. They all lived at home with their families, so I was drawn to find friends who understood what I was going through.

There were two best friends, one tiny and one tall, who were second-years and kind. I asked them questions occasionally. Lindsi, the tall one, is now a well-loved principal dancer with PNB. When Janece, the small one, had to leave at the end of the year, my heart broke for the friends. They had such a sweet bond.

Lesley, who received a company contract alongside Lindsi, was kind too. She has some of the most beautiful legs in the business, but back then they were still gaining strength. Sometimes, she'd complain, "My feet are just too flexible" or "My hyperextension makes everything harder!" I'm sure she was right, but it definitely made me jealous. I always did respect her, though. She worked hard and took her dancing seriously.

The boys were their own group. I love those boys even still, especially Kiyon Gaines, who must be one of PNBS' finest faculty members today.

Then there were the newbies, and we were divided into veteran PNB students and outsiders. The four outsiders were Jenny, Anne Yoon (whose name we only ever used in full for that entire first year), Kessa, and myself. At first, we hung around together, but then Jenny settled into other relationships. Kessa became my first friend, and we enjoyed a smattering of Anne Yoon in our lives.

Kessa, hailing from New Orleans, was fascinating. She lived with some random, volunteer host mother in an apartment in Northgate. Sometimes I drive past it and remember those days of being used by Kessa for my kindness and car rides. One night, Kessa talked me into driving her to a tattoo parlor in Ballard, Slave to the Needle. She wanted to have her boyfriend's name engraved on her butt. Going into it, she had a plan for possible break-up; she'd just have the bat-symbol put over it. This all sounded completely stupid to me, but I was so glad to have a friend who needed me that I nodded along AND paid for the thing (with assurances of reimbursement)! I should not have even been in the building. After the tat was done, while the artist was giving care instructions, Kessa fainted, and all these tough-looking tattoo parlor guys swarmed around her. She came-to almost as quickly as she went down, and one of them rattled on and on about blood sugar and pulled out a Dum-Dum to stick in her mouth. Then came the banter about ballerinas, our youth, and our flexibility that would become so familiar. The vibe was a strange and new mix of brotherhood and threat, and I started to push for us to get out of there.

After a couple of months, I realized that Kessa didn't care too much about me and that our relationship was one-sided, so I backed away. Kessa was the butt of a lot of joking that year. She was too different, and the rich girls were merciless.

Mockery is a special skill of the dancer set. Once, Drew aped my earnest preparation before a simple exercise at the barre. "Geez, Drew." I said. "Don't be a bitch. Some of us aren't as magically talented as you and have to take ourselves seriously from time to time."

"I'm sorry," said Drew, in total sincerity with a little shake of her head. "Mocking just comes so easy that sometimes I do it before I decide if it's a good idea." I loved her for saying that. She continued, "I think that's part of what makes me a good dancer, able to do lots of different kinds of things. It's all a version of mockery." She was wise for her age.

Another time, Kessa said to me, "I know why your body looks so weird; your arms are too short for it!" It took *years* for me to realize that was B.S.! Now every time someone wants a selfie-stick, I proudly go-go-Gadget my arm to its full, splendid length.

* * *

Our schedule at PNB included three classes per day taught by the teachers on staff; there were six teachers who taught us most often. Technique class happened every morning and always consisted of forty-five minutes of exercises at the barre and forty-five minutes dancing in "the center," meaning without the barres. We would then have a modern, pointe, or partnering class, and sometimes we would learn "variations," solos from existing ballets. Some days we had an additional technique class in the afternoon, or there were rehearsals where we would learn and practice whatever repertory would be performed next. Each of my years in the program, we had about twenty-five students in the group.

The teachers ranged from wonderful to average to miserable. Some of them were arrogant and condescending. The good ones were kind and encouraging. Fleming Halby was my favorite (and the only one who I'll call by his real name).

My least favorite classes were taught by the prima ballerina. Being a great dancer does not make someone a great teacher. She always said to us, "Just do it," as if everything should come as easily to us as it did to her. I much preferred more practical advice like "You are leaving your left shoulder behind in that turn" and "Press through your standing leg more to get height through your spine." I learned simple, basic things for the first time that I should have learned from Mrs. Hess, especially regarding pointe work. I had been told to "land softly" and "roll through," but finally at PNBS I learned how! Learning how to use my half vs. three-quarter pointe was a revelation! I lapped it all up, and my body and dancing changed for the better.

GOD STUFF

Have they counted the cost it'll take to bring down
All their earthly principles they're gonna have to abandon?
There's a slow, slow train comin' up around the bend

Bob Dylan
"Slow Train Coming" from *Slow Train Coming*

When I first moved, Aaron and I talked on the phone pretty
often. He had been accepted as an apprentice at Ballet Arizona,
so we were having similar experiences. My love-sickness over
him came to a major head, and I missed him desperately. I
constantly tried to tell him that I like-LIKED him, and he
constantly tried to steer the conversation away. Finally, he said
to me, "I love you, but Jessica I don't like girls."

"I know," I said, admitting it to myself after three years.

"You're my best friend."

"Yeah. I know," I said.

A few conversations later, we somehow started talking

about God and faith. I don't remember the lead in, but Aaron said, "Jessica, you can't actually believe that there's some God always watching, and that there's a 'for real' heaven and hell, right? It's ridiculous."

* * *

Throughout my childhood, I felt a lot of pressure. It seemed urgent to all the adults that I have "real faith." Every wrong move I made was evidence of the deeply backward, sinful heart I was taught that we all have. I learned that without God I was a hopeless, totally depraved mess. I stressed over my sinful habits; I tossed and turned at night agonizing over what my lustful, angry, and greedy thoughts meant about me. Why was it so hard for me to be good? How could God possibly want me? I knew about Jesus, but I was still so bad! When would I change? I just knew that God could not abide these things in me.

I knew I could not "earn my salvation" by good works. My church heavily emphasized grace as a theological concept, but it seemed like we all were still striving so desperately to have every answer and act all the right ways. The grace didn't seem to actually be as free as I was told. As a little girl, I was sure the grownups never sinned, and they kind of acted like that was the case.

By the time I was a teenager, I resented being sinned against by adults and rarely receiving apologies from them. There wasn't anything heinous, but it was enough to make me think that performance and perception perhaps mattered more than genuine goodness or faith. So I basically divided myself in two. There was Secret Cool Jessica who cussed and had a boyfriend, and there was Christian Homeschool Jessica who impressed adults and would be allowed to run off and chase a big dream. Neither version was fake, but they were both really stressed out.

Open rebellion was not an option. My plans were way too

big to risk losing my angel investors. And I didn't really want to rebel anyway. I did love God, and I believed he was real. I believed I was being held accountable to a higher purpose, but I also wanted to be more free than I was, to not have to work so hard to be perfect. At ballet, I was not embarrassed about being a good, little Christian girl, but I was worried that my church would not find acceptable the creeping desire to think outside of their boxes and go live in my own style of Christianity, one in which everyone could relax a little.

Moving to Seattle provided an opportunity for me to break away from the church if I wanted, but I had a reasonable fear that my parents would find out if I quit going to church and might yank my funding if I did. So when Aaron posed the question, "You can't really believe...," I gave my first wholehearted statement of faith.

"I don't know. All I know is I'm bad enough to deserve nothing, and I can never be good enough for God to let me be close to him. Jesus makes up for me." Taking my spiritual stand felt the same as telling Aaron I already knew he didn't like girls. Each statement had been true and known inside my heart long before I was able to wrap my cognitive mind around it.

We talked off and on for the next six months or so, and then Aaron faded into my past. Jesus, however, stuck around. The Christian life isn't really possible without him. I had been convinced for a long time that God was real, but I wasn't sure I liked him. I wanted the benefits—peace, eternal life, hope, et cetera; I didn't want the rules. Yet I couldn't escape the sense that if God wasn't different from me and didn't have standards of perfection, then what good was he? If I could bend him to be what I needed him to be, then he would be useless, not actually powerful at all.

I knew from Sunday School and my parents that Jesus makes a relationship with the holy, powerful, perfect God not only possible but safe and beneficial. If I wanted to really experience the benefits, peace, and freedom, then I needed the "relationship with Jesus" that I had been wanting but also avoiding my whole life. I knew I had to begin to see the rules and requirements as components of freedom. That was a real brain twister. I definitely could not continue living with the stress of duplicitousness. After that conversation on the phone with Aaron, I felt a shift inside and wanted badly to be one self all the time.

HOME LIFE

I need a phone call
I need a plane ride
I need a sunburn
I need a raincoat

Counting Crows
"Raining in Baltimore" from *August and Everything After*

The rain and darkness subtly depressed me, but the moodiness was fitting. I was lonely, but not hopeless, hesitant, but not scared. At my new home, I was happy, but never really comfortable. I loved my friend, the dancer son of my host family. I had some trouble connecting with the parents, but they were kind and easygoing.

The house was a huge, old mansion near St. Mark's Cathedral on Capitol Hill. Compared to the impeccable housekeeping of the Meador family, the place was a mess. The family was locked in some kind of battle with their neighbors who didn't like their new puppy barking too much outside. The solution was to keep the dog penned in the kitchen overnight where he peed all over the newspapers laid across the floor. Sometimes, a new layer of paper would be laid over the old one. I was so grossed out. One night I came in to see the dog drinking right out of the filtered water spigot like a hamster.

One night a couple months in, a visiting cousin of my host family came to have dinner and spend the night. He was Mormon and on a quick vacation before leaving for his "mission." He was in his twenties and was tall and broad shouldered. Right away when I was introduced, he gave me lots of attention. My friend, his sister, the cousin, and I took a walk to rent a movie. We picked *Monty Python and The Holy Grail* and talked music on the way back.

I sat next to the cousin on the couch to watch the movie, and when boredom finally drove away my friend, the cousin slid up to me and put his arm around me. I was so lonely and missed my friends back home so terribly. I needed the physical affection. But then I became uncomfortable as he pulled me tighter and tighter toward him, and I announced that I was going up to my room to go to bed. The attic space didn't have a lock, just a door at the base of an angled, railless staircase that wound up through the opening in the ceiling/floor. After a few minutes, the cousin came up into my room and said, "I brought some CDs for us to listen to."

"Oh, OK." I took the CD he held out and turned to put it in my CD player. When I turned around, he was sitting on my bed. I stayed on the other side of the room.

"Why don't you come lie down on this bed with me?" he said.

"No. You probably should go," I said.

"No, I don't think so," he said. "You're fine. Come on. It's gonna be OK," he said, and he laid back into my pillows.

"I want you to leave."

"Oh, calm down."

"Nope. I'm done. You need to get out."

"Fine." He slowly walked down my stairs.

I barely slept. I was so afraid he'd come back up, but I didn't feel like I could go talk to my host parents. The cousin was sleeping in my friend's room, or I would definitely have gone to tell him. I left without breakfast in the morning to avoid the cousin.

Later at the studio, I told my friend about what had happened, and that night his mother came to tell me how sorry she was and that what happened was not OK. Even though it wasn't a huge deal and certainly could have been worse, I think after that I just wanted to be somewhere I felt more secure, where I could have a lock.

I later told my parents about it, but at the time I didn't want them to know. It was just the kind of thing that I feared might push Mom on a mission to make me come home. Parental protectiveness can feel like a threat to a teenager. I liked it best when the threats were in their imaginations, not reality. I was highly motivated to keep reality looking peachy keen so that I could keep doing what I wanted.

I was young and coping with so many changes at once, and for the most part, I did it alone. Green Lake Presbyterian Church became an important, attractive place to me within just weeks. There I encountered liturgy, singing, and sermons that grabbed my attention and pulled me along. Songs like the *Gloria Patri* and statements of faith like "The Apostles' Creed" that I had known and recited my whole life suddenly had new meaning for me. The adults at Green Lake prayed for me in the middle of the room when I talked about my problems. Grown men talked about loving Jesus, and people stood up at evening services to confess sin *out loud*. The kind of Christianity I observed there made me want to draw closer; they made relationship with Jesus seem like a relief, not a burden.

At church one night, I told one of the moms that I wanted a new place to live, and a few weeks later, I moved into her spare bedroom. It wasn't perfect, but I was safe and felt more at home. The family was gracious, encouraging, and included me like I was their own. As soon as I turned eighteen that summer, my parents relented, and I got an apartment with some of my dancing classmates. I finally felt like a normal part of the PD program.

That first year was rough. I was behind training-wise and catching up socially. The second year was another story. I settled into a calm confidence. I was by no means the best dancer, probably not even one of the best, but I was well-liked. And I improved enough in my dancing to be regularly cast to dance with the *corps de ballet*. I danced in *The Sleeping Beauty, Don Quixote, Cinderella, The Merry Widow, Nutcracker,* and many other ballets that I hardly remember.

WESTERN SYMPHONY

Yes, everything was beautiful at the ballet
Hey! I was happy... at the ballet

Barbra Streisand
"At the Ballet"

Back in the day in Amarillo, Mr. Hess told me this story:

Alexia always worked hard; she would learn any part she could, even things that were not assigned to her. One fateful night at the New York City Ballet, she was in a rehearsal, and a dancer was injured. "Does anyone know her place?" the rehearsal director demanded. "I can do it," said the over-prepared Alexia. She danced it so well that she was allowed to have the part for the remainder of the season. And that is why you should always work hard. Hard work will pay off. You should be ready for any opportunity.

Mr. Hess employed these stories like Aesop's Fables, so I always wondered if they were really true. Still, though, I fantasized. I pictured myself in the scene, shiny leotard, all sweaty from practicing, saying, "I can do it!"

* * *

George Balanchine is, perhaps, the most famous choreographer of the last one hundred years. I read everything I could find about him and his company, New York City Ballet. I read through the catalog of his works many times. Even still, flipping through my books about him gives me the same flutter in my heart that other girls get for movie and rock stars (He did have a very Hollywood love life with five marriages.).

The Balanchine Centenary occurred around the time I came to Seattle, so companies were dancing even more of his work than usual. Pacific Northwest Ballet was directed at the time by Kent Stowell and Francia Russell, both of whom had danced for George Balanchine in his heyday. I hung on their every word, little devotee that I was. In the first year, I was cast to learn a couple of iconic Balanchine neoclassical works. I had seen them on PBS specials and read about them in books. One was *The Four Temperaments*, and I especially loved the tiny part I was given. All I did was jump on stage at the very end to do huge, forward, straight-legged kicks and exaggerated, hips-forward lunges. The large company of dancers on stage in that moment confirmed my sensation that I was finally part of the legacy I so longed to join.

We didn't do any neoclassical Balanchine in Amarillo. Instead we did a lot of very fun and spirited, but artistically questionable, mash-ups of country western dance mixed with ballet. The boys danced in boots and jeans, and the girls wore giant bows on our heads. Mr. Hess felt we needed to match the landscape and give people what they wanted. I'm not sure it's what they wanted, but we sure gave them a lot of it. I always felt a little embarrassed by our shows and wished we could do "real" ballet, the ballets I read about. I soaked up every chance I had to learn Balanchine's or other classic choreography while I was studying with companies over the summers or by borrowing videos from the library. I'm sure I wore out lots of videotape with my constant stopping, rewinding, and replaying. Finally, at PNB, I learned things properly, and I was cast to learn a *corps de ballet* position in *Western Symphony*, a cowboy/ballet mash-up by Balanchine himself.

Western Symphony was created in 1954 to music specially commissioned from Hershey Kay, an American composer. He used traditional western folk tunes and songs to create the base for his twangy, orchestral score. Saloon-girl-styled costumes by Balanchine's famed costume designer, Karinska, were added the next year along with an Old West stage setting. Balanchine loved America, and *Western Symphony* is a sign of that love.

I was only an understudy, but I learned the part and practiced it as well as I could without ever getting to actually dance it along with everyone else. As a student, being an understudy was a privilege. The understudy's name would be listed off to the side of the person being given the role on the casting lists. Understudies have tickets to the practice studio and all the theater rehearsals.

It isn't unusual to need to "go in" as an understudy, but generally we expected not to be needed. We were required to show up to the theater early and check to see whether any last-minute changes had been made, but after "Places!" was called, we could go home. I usually went to the box office to get a comp ticket then found my seat to watch the company perform. Many of the other students in my division had spent years around professional companies and performance, but I had not. I wanted to catch up. *Western Symphony* was the first piece on the bill, and I settled into my seat in the last row of the orchestra section seating.

I loved watching *Western*. It is an engaging, entertaining

ballet. I especially loved it because it felt like I was watching what Mr. Hess had been trying to figure out: how to combine the spirit of the Old West and ballet. The fact that George Balanchine himself had enough affection for cowboys to make a ballet around the subject seemed to validate Mr. Hess's attempts. By my math, *Western* legitimized my prior training, and I felt a deep sense of pride in my Texas roots. While I had fantasized throughout my Texas childhood about a New York City, neoclassical life, I could see that Balanchine, at least a little bit, had fantasized about and romanticized the place I was raised. He was often even photographed wearing a bolo tie. So was Mr. Hess.

As I mused over these things and watched the show, I was shaken from my reverie by something going wrong on stage. One of the newest members of the corps fell at the end of a scene and was clearly unable to get up on her own. Her partner pulled her up and off the stage. She was not dancing the part that I knew, so I stayed in my seat.

A moment later, I felt a tap on my shoulder. "Come on!" a classmate, Reid, whispered, and we ran from the back of the house through the passageway to backstage. "They need you to do her place because the other understudies all went home; you're the opposite!" Lots of ballet is symmetrical, and had I been on stage, I would have been dancing the mirror image to the girl who fell.

"I can do it!" I said. And, though there was no joy at Kylee's injury, my heart was set to rupture with glee at my luck. I immediately started running through the steps in my mind and noting which direction to go, which leg to use. It would be all completely opposite to what I had practiced.

The Artistic Director herself was waiting to talk to me, "Now, you just pay attention, and the dancers will help you." I had no time to be afraid as I was rushed to the dressing room and put into a pair of black tights and a costume. I didn't have any requisite black pointe shoes, so another dancer my size gave me some of hers that didn't have ribbons attached. We hastily safety-pinned the ribbons, and they smoothed my hair into the best bun we could manage. As I ran down to the stage, my heart was fluttering. I was full of adrenaline and bursting with joy. "Here," whispered Lindsi as she scrawled red lipstick onto my face.

It was a perfect storm: Texan me, George Balanchine, Mr. Hess's stories flaming to life all around me, and beautiful *Western Symphony*. I'm sure I made technical mistakes. I'm sure I looked a fright at times, but I smiled wide, almost maniacally, as I went through the motions.

One of the steps and the feeling of performing it will be in my body forever. The step is called *ballotte*. Springing into the air, both legs are drawn up under the body, knees to the side, ankles together with pointed toes. Upon landing on one leg, the opposite leg extends. In *Western Symphony*, Balanchine has the dancers *ballotte* like they are at a hoedown: legs up! One front! Legs up! One back! And repeat, repeat, repeat. It is a happy, happy dance and, though I remember it being so much harder than I thought it would be, it felt natural to me, Amarillo Girl. I would never have been caught dead going all rodeo-style and dancing like that, but because Balanchine had asked me to, I did it with gusto.

I never had to dance the position I was thrust into that night again, but with the shuffling of dancers I was able to perform in the rest of the shows in the original position I had learned. Theater policy was changed at that point to require under-studies to remain at the theater until the ballets were completed. Whenever it was mentioned, I would squeal a bit inside that I was the one who had stayed. It was my experience that changed everything. I had a story to tell Mr. Hess, one that he could then tell about me. I felt humbled by how pitiful I probably was on stage that night, but the fact that it happened gave me great hope that some of Mr. Hess's other Alexia stories would also transfer to me.

OFFSTAGE

Every move you make...
I'll be watching you

The Police
"Every Move You Make" from *Synchronicity*

The Professional Division program is an excellent system with a balance of training and performance opportunities. At the end of my second year, I was invited to Los Angeles with the company to dance a portion of *A Midsummer Night's Dream* at the Hollywood Bowl. Only six students were included, and we were treated well by the company members. I had a ball dancing on the stage where once The Beatles had played, and kept telling myself: "This is happening NOW. It may never happen again!"

I was one of Hippolyta's Hounds and had the pleasure of whacking my side extension on *grand battement a la seconde* while wearing a brown unitard and a pretty realistic looking beagle head. We had to pay our dues. Stage time isn't free when you're a newbie, and embarrassing costumes were often the fee. Julie Andrews herself attended the performance. She was allowed to exit through the stage gate, and on her way out, we ambushed her. Lindsi, who was in the company at that point, said, "You're Mary Poppins!" I was so embarrassed. Still, we all begged the guy who was with her to take photos with our disposable cameras. I thought he looked familiar at the time and have since concluded that he was Gary Marshall. That explains how he took such a great photo on a disposable camera!

All that fun costs money. To be a dancer is to be "on" all the time. You represent the ballet everywhere you go. Ballet is expensive, so directors are always fundraising. As students, some of us had a "Named Donor," a person who paid our tuition, stipend, or some combination. We would go to receptions to thank our donors, and by the last year, I was often given the opportunity to give a quick little speech prompted by "What does your donor mean to you?"

Then there were the big galas and soirees where company members would do the schmoozing and groups of students were there to wear costumes and pose for photos. I always felt half-naked at those things. Fancy people dressed to the nines, drunk on cocktails would slur their greetings or condescension to us.

When #metoo became useful, my first thoughts were of being directly sexually harassed in a coffee shop where I worked. But then I remembered those donor events and all the times I was touched, leered at, or asked a hundred times how flexible I was by bored, wandering husbands. Men always asked the stupid flexibility question as though they were the first one to think of it. I loved being invited to the events, though. I'd show up for anything to have a chance to be seen as useful—preferably indispensable—to the company.

At an event titled "Russian Nights," a fellow peon, the

waiter passing *hors d'oeuvres,* sidled up to me every time he had something new on the tray. I tasted caviar for the first time and was blown away. He flirted all night, bringing me caviar and secret sips of "expensive" champagne, but I was clueless. I was so convinced that I was second-class that it never occurred to me that anyone, even this caviar guy, could possibly be interested in me.

When the parties were held at the studios, we would get particularly excited. Receptions and fundraisers meant there would be leftover food in the student lounge fridge the next day. More importantly, the braver among us had become good at sneaking in to steal bottles of wine. There's no party like a dancer party! For the first six months of my time in Seattle, I partied. But that tender conscience of mine, the one that just *had* to tell Mom about smoking cigarettes, kicked in pretty quickly.

Also the "relationship with Jesus" thing was beginning to matter more to me. So I decided that following the law of the land in terms of drinking age was a good step. I stayed dry from then on, but I still went to the parties and had a great time. (Can this Goody-Two-Ballet-Shoes be for real? Yep. For real, y'all.)

Some friends and I crashed a massive Mardi Gras party in a mansion on Queen Anne Hill just because we saw it. The fire dancers on the lawn had drawn us up the block, and the chocolate fountains sucked us in the door. We danced and laughed inside for a long time until a man asked us if we were from the ballet. He told us he was on the board and that he was perfectly happy to keep our secret if we wanted to keep spending time with him. We quickly extracted ourselves and kept to our own parties after that.

All our shenanigans bonded us, and we were very loyal to our friends. But we were definitely cliquey. There was an air of superiority among us, and due to the competitive nature of our business, we could be very judgmental and selfish.

Most of us dealt with some amount of internal distress. Mental health issues were common: Disordered Eating, Obsessive-Compulsive Disorder, Depression, Anxiety. I definitely didn't come out unscathed, but I mercifully dodged some of the big bullets.

Matters of the body can also be insurmountable for some dancers. If it isn't weight, height, "beauty," or flexibility (things that genetics have almost entirely predetermined), then it's strength, predisposition to illness or injury, or the ubiquitous fear of rejection. Dancers know and say things about themselves and each other like "horse teeth," "big-head," "biscuit feet;" if it isn't perfect, it's fair game.

The industry standards are extreme and exclusive. I reached out to one of my best friends from PNB, Carla, to ask what she remembered about the stress level in those days. Here's part of what she wrote:

> I think I was experiencing some pretty chronic anxiety the two years I was in Seattle. Anxiety which colored my interactions with other people. I remember feeling safe with you and Reid, but otherwise I felt like I needed to keep up a boundary so I wouldn't feel the complete impact of the pressure that was constant. We had to keep going and not complain because if we couldn't do it then someone else could. The indifference of the teachers and directors is what finally made me crave a different life. I don't think I could have stood another decade or two of the self-doubt. Even with the doses of joy on stage.

Carla was beautiful, talented, kind, well-trained, well-liked, well-spoken, and thoughtful. She articulated the most painful aspect of the stress with this sentence: "The indifference of the teachers and directors is what finally made me crave a different life."

Scrutiny without care is a dangerous scalpel—accurate,

exact, but not healing. Every teacher is different, but back then none of them seemed to truly care about us. There was no Mr. Hess. Carla and I agreed that we were waiting for someone to mentor us, to pull us under a wing and show us the path to greatness. We wanted to be noticed, but we wanted to be noticed for who we were and what we could bring to the company, even the world! Instead, most of the time the attention we received was not really about us. It was about making the ballet look right. I find it very sad. We were a room full of exceptional, driven, creative people, typically being reduced to scenery.

At the ballet and because of the ballet, I couldn't fully relax. I was always glad to have outside relationships at my church and at my part-time job at the coffee shop where I often made lattes for Dave Matthews. Green Lake Pres was full of people who were creating art and decimating some of the norms of the Christian culture of Texas to which I was accustomed.

Nathan Partain was my favorite of these people. He was Chief Musician at Green Lake Pres. He wrote songs, made visual art, had a ponytail, smelled like patchouli, and hardly ever wore shoes. Nathan could sing original, personal lyrics to God and about God in front of everyone while pounding the hand drums. And the pastors let him! Nathan recognized me as an artist and gave me entry into the arts culture at the church. I still think of him as a big brother. The way Nathan and the other Christian artists treated me was lightyears different than the treatment of the ballet. He said hard things to me sometimes, but he said them with love. When he married Sarah, she became my big sister, and I spent lots of time at their house, a giant, old craftsman right next to our church building.

I don't remember ever feeling responsible for pleasing them or meeting expectations, explicit or implicit, and they were endlessly kind and inclusive. They seemed to embody this goal of mine—to just be myself, be the Elise, be a Christian, and be an artist.

HAPPY TULIP DAY

Come and tell me what you're thinking
'Cause just when the boat is sinking
A little light is blinking
And I will come and rescue you

The White Stripes
"Apple Blossom" from *De Stijl*

My first year in Seattle I was invited by Nathan's friend, one of the pastors, to attend a youth group retreat for Green Lake Pres. The dates worked out with my class and performance schedule, and I took my first trip to Canada. We went to Salt Spring Island in the spring, and I got pushed into a cold lake by a boy. Later, I learned he had a crush on me. I wasn't interested in the slightest but was intrigued by someone else, Brendan, who had stayed away from the dock because he couldn't swim. Later that night, around a fire, I took a good, long look at the nonswimmer.

We had discussed music before, and he had impressed me. Part of the appeal of Seattle for a girl from Amarillo was the prevalence of great musical taste; "great" meaning "played on the college music station I worshiped back home and not country." I wasn't interested in him then. I was pretty sure he was a pothead, what with his Nirvana t-shirts and bleach-blonde grown-out hair, and that held no appeal for me. At the campfire, though, he showed his seriousness, his thoughtfulness, and I started to pay attention. He didn't seem to need to people-please at all.

On the ferry home, a group of girls asked if I liked him. I cooly answered the only right answer: "I don't know," even though I did know. "He says he likes you," they giggled. At some point during that long ferry ride in unseasonably warm sunshine, he and I nonchalantly found each other and used the wooden beads I had purchased at the terminal to make matching necklaces. I don't think either one of us took them off for months.

The first time he called me, he framed it as a courtesy call to let me know that Coldplay would be playing at Benaroya Hall in June. I considered this a flag-waving of his interest because it was only April, and he must want to keep in touch at least until this concert. We planned to go. By that point I was pretty googly-eyed over him, but I was still wondering if I would ever be able to get over the fact that I was taller.

On April 25th, 2001, a Wednesday, I swung by the coffee shop to kill some time and consult with my college-aged fellow employees, sage in their old age. I was getting tired of the lack of definition in my relationship with this new boy. They dutifully teased me, but Brian said that I should definitely keep trying to hang out with him and see what happened. I knew that Brendan worked at an Arby's near his house, so I decided to casually pop in that night. It was a thirty-minute drive, and I remember how excited and jittery I felt as I picked my way there using the map from my glove box.

Two things changed forever for me the moment I walked into the Arby's: the smell of curly fries and the potential for forest-green polo shirts to be attractive attire. As I came through the double-glass doors, Brendan was exiting the swinging door that led out from behind the counter. We nearly walked into each other, and his jaw dropped open. I can still see him standing there in black Dockers, the Arby's polo, a name tag, and his yellow-blonde shaggy hair. His long-lashed eyes sparkled at my sudden appearance, and I knew for sure that it was just a matter of time. We sat together while he ate his crispy chicken concoction slathered in honey mustard.

I drove him up the hill to his house. Sadly, it was a school night, so I had to go. Brendan was a junior in high school. His parents suggested he walk me to my car, the red, Saturn station wagon. The giant bubble of LIKE was pushing from inside me to the point of popping, but I wanted him to tell me first. Instead, he reached down to the tulips growing alongside the driveway. He pulled his house key from his pocket and messily tore through the stem of a red one. Holding it out to me, he said, "My mom said I could give this to you."

"Aw, that's so sweet," I answered and took the flower. Having never thought much of tulips before, they immediately became my favorite. No more words came out of either of us. We said goodbye, and I drove away. My car smelled like curly fries, and I sang Coldplay at the top of my lungs. One tulip petal is still left in my box of memorabilia.

Now we laugh, and Brendan defends himself for delivering the line about his mother's permission. He just wanted me to know he wasn't being inconsiderate. Two nights after the tulip delivery, he did finally tell me he liked me, and he began with, "Remember the other night when I gave you the flower...." I have loved remembering the night he gave me the flower ever since.

He didn't sweep me off my feet in an artsy, romantic way like Calvin had, and he cannot dance to save his life. But he is a great writer, and he gave me a few poems, some of which were very beautiful.

I found out later that my favorite poem had originally been written about another girl! When he realized I was hurt, he was confused. "Well," he said, "I just figured it was a poem I wrote for a girl I liked, and now that's you. So the poem is for you." Classic Brendan. Logic and rational thinking outweighed emotion, and sometimes relational sensitivity. But he was not cold. Music, lyrics, literature, movies, dead squirrels on the road all could make him cry. He was easily, tenderly moved by beauty, loss, and mercy.

Calvin had been romantic and naturally knew how to say just what I wanted to hear; Brendan worked on a different level. He never was infatuated or motivated by romantic idealism. I sometimes wished he was! But we romantic types come with insecurity and a mercurial nature—hence Calvin's intense spite for me after we broke up. I didn't really want someone who thought just like I did. I was attracted to Brendan because of his calm, consistent, deep-thinking nature. He cared for me with a level of friendship and equality that I had never experienced. We were young, but I had always leaned toward being serious about things.

Early in our dating, he was "a keeper," but he also turned out to be *my* keeper. He looked after me. Once we were at Target, and I thought I'd be funny and run up the down escalator. I fell very hard at the top scraping my knee and making my wrist sore. Even though I was hurting, I immediately laughed and looked up at him ready to crack a joke. There was no humor in his eyes. He didn't find it funny in the slightest. Genuinely concerned, he took my hands and helped me up; he looked right into my eyes and asked, "Are you OK?" Here was a friend who would love me even if I fell, even when I was an idiot. There was no, "Well, that's what you get, dummy!" He was unique.

LADLES AND LIP SYNC

Ooh, see that girl
Watch that scene

ABBA
"Dancin' Queen" from *Arrival*

I was having the time of my life during the second of three years as a Professional Division student. I had already been told I would have a third year as a PD. Most dancers did two, but I started on the young end and needed the extra time of refinement. I came to PNB a raw little ball of flexibility and eagerness, but I didn't have much training in the finer points of technique. The promise of that third year made my second a breeze.

About half of my good friends, though, were under intense pressure. They needed to figure out their next steps. They were coming up on the big moment when they would find out whether all their work had paid off and they would be doing what they loved for at least another year. Dancing is a one-season-at-a-time kind of gig. You never know when your contract will be dropped or you might be injured and have the whole dream vaporize.

It was 2002, the spring following 9-11, and arts companies across the country were losing donors in the economic downturn. The previous spring, we had the opportunity to be seen by directors from across the country, and it was reasonable for someone from a program like ours to expect to get a contract somewhere. This year? Not so much. We were nervous. There just weren't as many jobs available. Add to this worry about jobs the usual stresses of being a dancer: aches and pains, making enough money, keeping your body in shape (AKA stay skinny), and the constant wonder of whether the directors and teachers still like and approve of you. Tensions could run pretty high in the studios.

All this pressure forged simultaneously deep but sometimes volatile relationships. The people around you were your biggest, most direct threats and competition, and yet they were also the only people in the world who really knew what you were going through. Kari, who once intimidated me, eventually became my roommate. Of all the dancers, I still see her now and then and love her most dearly.

Being entertainers, we always had a wild ton of fun. There were few secrets among us. We pretty much knew each other's business just because we were never apart. It was an everyone-PMS-on-the-same-week kind of female community. (Well it was for those of us who had a BMI that could support reproductive ability!). There just isn't a closeness like the closeness of friends who get dressed and undressed in the same locker room multiple times a day. We supported each other through injuries and illnesses that we often were trying to conceal from the powers that be.

Every day we danced our hearts out in the studios and wore out our bodies too. There may have been sniping remarks made. There may have been hurt feelings over casting lists going up. We might have been scolded for talking to each other too much. Maybe one of us was being favored over the rest. But in spite of myriad reasons to want a break from each other, generally my group of about seven close friends was always ready to get home and play together. We needed each other. Life was stressful, and our families were thousands of miles away. So what would we do after dancing eight hours a day? Well, we would dance of course.

Our nightly agenda went something like this:

1. Watch *Friends* reruns.

2. Order pizza, make pasta, or cook something else cheap together.

3. Dance party.

The dance partying included free-for-all time and a more organized section of lip-sync performances. There was always a dash for the kitchen to find a microphone. I remember there were a couple of kitchen utensils we especially wanted to use, like that prong-sided spoon one uses for serving spaghetti— now THAT's a makeshift microphone. Almost always, this scene went down in Drew and Anne (Yoon)'s apartment. They had a spot close to the studios, but more than that I think they had the gravitas required to be a home base. Stayce and I lived up at the top of Queen Anne Hill, and she was the one person with a car making it possible for us to get home without walking.

The soundtrack of our evenings varied some but very little. Aqua (yes, that band that sang the Barbie song) and ABBA were our mainstays. We were just having fun, but there was something pretty deep and magical about "Dancing Queen." It was OUR song. We were the dancing queens. Like little hipster predecessors in Lower Queen Anne, we were technically listening to and loving this stuff with a pinch of irony. But I think each of us was hoping she was the real Dancing Queen, never mind the fact that most of us were eighteen.

* * *

The on-stage tomfoolery got pretty ridiculous sometimes. One long *Nutcracker* season somebody bought a remote-controlled fart-noise machine. We hid it in the party scene set and then got the best abdominal workout of our lives. But my favorite moments were the ones we didn't plan, like the first night of *Chaconne.*

Bourée is not kind to an exposed butt cheek (even if it is made of steel), and Drew had no time to fix her costume. It was on backward, an easy (I guess?) mistake to make with the double-scoop-necked, light brown leotard and thin skirt. As we say in the classy world of ballet, her ass was out. We were dancing an ethereal piece of work in which dancers float and change like wisps of cloud. We set a peaceful scene for the soloists as we *bouréed* from formation to swirl to formation. The curtain swooshed silently into the fly space to reveal eight beautiful, teenage dancers, one with wardrobe malfunction.

The music calmed our bouncing, muffled tittering, and we did our best to behave like professional dancers. That night was one of many narrow escapes. Nervous laughter is my nemesis. Finally bouréeing into the wings I dropped my head back with relief. SAFE! I hadn't ruined the scene. Each hilarious experience and every ballet tightened another knot in our little friendship bracelets, but we all had worked way too hard to screw it up for a laugh no matter how badly it was needed.

* * *

I miss those days the same way anyone misses her favorite teenage pastimes. I have many wonderful friends right now. I have friends who have watched me give birth. I have friends who have told me their saddest, most horrific memories. I have confessed things to some of my current friends that I thought I would never say aloud. And yet somehow I still don't feel as close to these women I have now as I did to my Professional Division friends. I hardly ever talk to most of those girls now, but I could without a doubt pick right up where we left off. These are treasured relationships for most people, the childhood friendships that last forever.

My life is big now. I have four children, a husband, a home, a dog, volunteer positions, illness, et cetera. In some ways, my stresses have increased. I have *many* more lives to worry about now, so many opportunities to make giant, life-changing mistakes. But somehow I still feel like those days in the studios were more pressured. And yet I never sweated things then, because we danced together. We did our favorite thing together and laughed for hours. Oh, how I wish I could still do that now! Sometimes, I will dance party with the kids, and it definitely scratches the itch, just not enough to make it go away.

CONTRACT

I am waiting for something to go wrong
I am waiting for familiar resolve

Death Cab for Cutie
"Expo '86" from *Transatlanticism*

From what I gathered, my usefulness to PNB was threefold:

- I was exactly the right size and had no trouble with my weight.
- I could keep up in rehearsals and steadily improved.
- I was optimistic and cheerful; the right kind of normal.

If the staff or teachers had a question or idea for the students, they would run it through me. If my class needed a break or schedule change, I was the representative. In times of stress around performances or auditions, I was rock-solid. I smiled. I cracked jokes; I didn't complain. Dancers regularly engaged in hallway hysteria. I never could tell if they were performance art, panic attacks, immaturity, or some combination of the three. But I didn't throw fits. I was the Elise.

Every time a new, clean piece of white paper went up on our bulletin board, we'd flock and gawk. The murmur would travel, "casting is up," and everyone would crowd to see if and where her last name was listed. By the third year, my name was always where I wanted it to be, and I stayed grateful even after I stopped being surprised.

My "spots" for *Nutcracker* were great. *Nutcracker* was our chance to show that we looked good with the company and should be given contracts. During our second-to-last theater rehearsal, a few teachers were there to watch along with the regularly attending Artistic Director and Ballet Masters. I was dancing my spot as a "company flower," a dancer in a position reserved for company members (and some PDs) in the "Waltz of the Flowers." The choreography was much more difficult and fun than for "school flowers," the other half of the dancers. My "Co-Flo" spot was right in the front, and I was having a ball dancing it. The choreography was swooping, leaping, running fun on stage. It was cheerful, friendly, and challenging enough to feel like an accomplishment.

After the rehearsal, I ran into two different teachers on my way out. Each one of them said to me, "You were looking really good in "Flowers." Keep that up!" One also said, "Really, you were beautiful. I know they're going to be watching you a lot this run." Then the Ballet Mistress said, "Jessica, you were so great up there! Really nice work. Keep doing that."

THREE. Three unsolicited compliments. It wasn't nothing. In a world where power and posturing are tools, a true compliment meant a lot.

The next morning, I called my mom to tell her about it. I rehearsed to her all the reasons I could expect to get a job in January. I was dancing well, getting good parts, and attracting positive attention. Every time we talked, I could feel my parents' excitement and relief. The gamble I had begged them to take was likely to pay off. We had every reason to believe that when I began auditioning in January I would find a job, and for the first time ever, I thought I may even have a chance at PNB. I timidly let myself think maybe I could be one of the two or three who would be offered full-time employment in the spring.

Thank God those three spoke up. My performance of Kent Stowell's down-stage-right company flower turned out to be the best dancing of my life.

THE ACCIDENT

There'll always be a few things, maybe several things
That you're going to find really difficult to forgive

The Mountain Goats
"Up The Wolves" from *The Sunset Tree*

In 2002, the Seattle Opera House was being remodeled to become Marion Oliver McCaw Hall, so we danced up the street at the temporary Mercer Arts Arena. *Nutcracker* was the one exception and would be performed at the Paramount Theater downtown. The PD dressing room was about half the size of the one at the Opera House, but it was still four flights up.

The night of our final dress rehearsal, I was riding high from the compliments on the prior rehearsal. We bantered and made up our faces. Everyone had her own little tricks: a little white eyeliner for the inner corner, two black wings to extend the lashes, glitter on the brow bone, shimmer dust on the *decollete*. I liked doing my eyes. I have a wide space between my lash line and brow, lots of canvas to shadow. But, my favorite trick was contouring my red lips by highlighting with a pale pink, high-shimmer gloss.

Everyone in the dressing room picked up the pace as ten-minute and then five-minute calls were made. Since this was our final dress rehearsal, we'd have a full audience of donors and benefit ticket recipients. I would dance Moors (the "Spanish Dance") in Act II and Nurse in Act I. It was an easy show for me (no pointe shoes!), yet I was nervous. I felt like an idiot there in the dressing room, unaccustomed to stage fright. I didn't even know to call the trilling, ruminating thoughts and pounding, dizzying heart "anxiety." I was nervous over one of the easiest parts in the whole show, a part I had performed for two years already, Clara's Nurse. But the previous year, during my last performance of Nurse, I had tripped on the set stairs and fell at the bottom. Going into the new season, I was rattled and worried it would happen again.

"Places!" was called, and a little bolt of electricity shot through my heart. I went to stage right and tucked myself into my hidey-hole on the set. The first dancing (pantomiming mostly) of the show happened outside the very outer scrim on the narrow apron of stage. The scrim itself had a window cut out of its middle about six or seven feet off the ground. Inside the window, an 8' by 8'ish square vignette of Clara's bedroom was nestled like a shadow box. A scrim is different than a curtain. A scrim can be transparent, translucent, or opaque depending on where light is hitting it.

"Little Clara," the tween dancer who played Clara for the first few scenes slept in the little bed, tossing and turning with a bad dream. Down on the stage below, characters acted out her nightmare of being attacked by a rat. The trick of showing Clara inside the little window was accomplished by having a wide but shallow platform pressed directly against the scrim. The stairs leading from the bedroom-scene platform down to the stage had a wall on one side and a drop on the other. The staircase was about eighteen inches wide while my gown's skirt and petticoat made me two feet wide. I scooched my tiny butt in a big skirt onto the second or third step from the bottom between the wall of the platform piece and the scrim. I sat there silently praying that I wouldn't trip again coming down those stairs.

With his overture for *The Nutcracker*, Tchaikovsky captured the anticipatory excitement of a child's heart. For dancers, the overture carries not simply the Christmas party joy that the story requires but all the thrill of putting on a show. The audience, eager for the curtain to go up, whether they've seen it once or a dozen times, feels it. Little girls in itchy, beautiful dresses squirming in seats and being shushed for saying, "Where are the ballerinas?" can feel it too. There in my quiet corner of the stage, for the first time in my life, the overture had some words: "Bah, bum, bah, bum, bump, bump, bah. Please, don't let me fall, God." I turned it into a bouncy ditty and tried to josh myself out of my silly overreaction to tripping the year prior. I thought about being seven years old and waiting to be the first body on stage, my tiny hands tucked into a purple velvet muff.

A final "plink, plank, Plunk" ended the overture, and the gliding, silvery violins invited bodies onto the stage and the audience to sit back and enjoy the show. I stood up and turned around to look up the stairs toward Clara fretting in her stage sleep. I crept up a few more steps clutching a prop dress in my hand and stayed just out of the viewers' sight. Finally, Clara popped to sitting, waking suddenly from her dream. That was my cue, and I bustled up the stairs to appear in the window with her. "C'mon, Clara! How can you still be napping?! Guests will arrive any moment, and you need to be in this dress!" I said it all with large movements and facial expressions, trying to communicate all the way to the third tier seating. I swooped Clara along in front of me to go down the stairs first.

Just a few steps down, I felt a bump and jostle, an earthquake just for me and little Clara. She was almost to the bottom and managed to leap off to the wing. I, still five feet up the staircase, tried to fight my body's sway to the left as the platform was jerked to the right, but the momentum of the set piece being run full-speed off the stage threw me over the side toward the scrim.

As I fell, time slowed down enough for me to see the Stage Manager's and dancers' eyes widen with alarm. The sidelights were bright, and my bonnet ties flew up into my sticky, perfect lipgloss. "Well, so much for not tripping," I thought.

I couldn't believe that after all my silly *Sturm and Drang* there had actually been something real to worry about. "What is happening?" flashed in my mind.

And then I heard an answer from somewhere else in my body, from lower down than my brain, "I'm letting you fall." Then the ground slammed into me, my feet and shins taking the brunt of it then my hands and forearms hitting too. Shock and shame inundated my whole body, and I did not want to be seen on my hands and knees when that scrim flew up. I scrambled to my feet and ran into the wings completely bewildered. Someone had screwed up, and it wasn't me.

"Are you OK?" Stage Manager said.

"Ummm, I think so. I smacked my leg and foot pretty hard." I lifted up the fluffy layers of my petticoat. Blood was seeping through the pink tights on the top of my foot.

"Ooh. Do you need a Band-Aid?"

"I'm fine I think."

"OK. Well let me know."

I just wanted to get away. I felt true clinical shock settle into my bones and guts; my lungs tightened. I did not want to cry there backstage and went jogging along the back passageway behind the stage to get to the stairs to my dressing room. Already berating myself, I thought, *Geez, calm down. It's OK. Could have been a lot worse. You probably did it to yourself by being all weird and nervous about tripping. But I didn't trip. The crew did it. Still, doesn't matter. Don't make it a thing.*

Despite my brain's best efforts, the crying was inevitable and could not be stopped. My friends had thinned in the dressing room because many were down doing the party scene or getting their pointe shoes ready for Snow. I took a minute to use the corner of a folded paper towel to surgically remove tears from my ducts the moment they emerged. I couldn't let them smear my makeup; I had more appearances as Nurse.

When the party scene was finally over, I went back up, let the dresser remove my dress, then sat down on the ground, my character shoes on my feet sticking out in front of me. My shin was throbbing, and the Band-Aids I'd gone back to get from Stage Manager showed under the blood stain on my tights. An awkward, unwanted sob gurgled it's way out, and the hot tears made their streaks through my eyeliner and foundation.

"Oh, Jessica! What's wrong?" My friends came around me.

"I fell doing Nurse."

"That's OK! Was it bad?"

"Oh, no one from the audience saw, but I'm all freaked out."

"Are you hurt?"

"No. Well, yeah. Kind of. My leg...."

"Oooh, yeah. Kinda swollen."

"I'm sure it's just bruised."

They tried to cheer me up, and we changed into our Second Act costumes. Down on the stage, behind the lowered curtain, we all sat to warm up and quietly chat. The Artistic Director herself came to find me. It was not a chance encounter. She came straight to me and asked if I was alright. "I think it's just some bruising," I said as she ran her grandmotherly touch over the bluish swell of my shin showing through my tights. "Well, be sure to check in with the PT." The Stage Manager had walked over too, and the Artistic Director looked up to ask her, "What happened here?"

"Well, I think we're still just getting used to the new space.

That transition is so tight in the smaller theater, and they were pushing to get it done in time."

The two women walked over to a knot of stagehands in the middle of the stage. One of them was Murphey. I didn't know him, but I think I knew his name already. I can't recall if I learned it later on or if maybe it was right then as I tried to eavesdrop on their conversation. From what I gathered, he had made the call to strike the piece. To "strike" is to remove a set-piece from the stage, and in my case, Murphey made a bad call. He should have had confirmation that no people remained on the piece. With no railing, there was no way for us to be safe if it moved. There was a lot of nodding, and the Artistic Director turned her head to look at me over her shoulder. I quickly looked down toward my leg and pulled myself into a forward bend, stretching out my hamstrings. I felt so pleased to have her care for just that tiny moment.

No one ever apologized.

ART SUPPLIES

There's a limit to your love
Your love, your love, your love

Feist
"Limit to Your Love" from *The Reminder*

Today, in 2018, my daughter, Hazel Belle, is dancing her way through her first modern dance class while I type. She took pre-ballet and a ballet/tap combo when she was younger, but on a sad day when she just couldn't deal with tights or shoes another minute, she tearfully decided that ballet was not for her. Hazel Belle's former teacher let me know that HB was old enough to switch to modern. NO TIGHTS. Problem solved! My little dancey dolly squealed and bounced when I told her. I did my own internal squealing too! Seeing her love music and movement is satisfying enough, but she gets to have a costume and be in the annual recital. I will get at least ONE backstage moment with a kid. I hope the teacher picks a costume poor HB can stand.

Because that's just it: as a dancer, you don't get many choices. You may choose a style, a studio, a teacher, but beyond the continually made decision to keep going or to quit, that's all. It killed me to watch HB struggle between her heart's desire to dance and her body's inability to cope with the sensations of the uniform. She was only five years old and already the rules were screwing her over! I, her hardcore, ballet student mother, could only say, "Sorry, baby. That's how it is."

I can't speak to all the disciplines, but I know about ballet. Staunchly held beliefs and reasoning justify every rule and restriction. Tights and leotards allow the instructor to see how the muscles are working. Wispy hair in the face and dangling ponytails interfere with the ability to learn turning properly. Turn-out? Of course. Pointed toes? A must. Jewelry? It may shoot your eye out. *Pliés* before *tendues* before *degage* before *rond de jambe en l'air*, and why would you ever dream of doing differently? These days, plenty of boundaries are being pushed, and many a college dance department prides itself on trying to unmake and redesign the rules and norms. But ballet just wouldn't be the same without the structure.

I don't know many young dancers who get into it for the rules, though.

Me? I loved the feeling of flying across the room and of an audience's gaze. Applause wasn't half bad, and if I could eke a "Good!" out of Mrs. Camille Hess, all the better. Soon I learned that the more I followed the rules, the more the teachers paid attention to me. Practicing lightened my heart, filled my imagination, invigorated my body, and endorphin-flooded my brain. Bit by bit, I made the connections: listen carefully + follow the rules + practice = dance better. Dance better = get better spots in the studio and in the dances. Take more classes + put up with more screaming and abuse = get bigger parts.

To be a dancer is to know how best to please teachers and

directors. The more you look, behave, and dance the way they want, the more opportunities you are given. Those few hours on stage are worth weeks and months in the studio. In a regular class, a "That's it!" or "Yes! Good!" from a person in power can fuel a dancer for a week. People-pleasing, performing, beating my body, and enjoying my body all rolled into one big, complicated system of psychological cause and effect.

When it's working, it's great. You stay strong, you stay skinny, you stay pretty, and they love you. "Keep it together" is the mantra because when you start to fall apart, it doesn't take long for dancer/teacher/choreographer/director relationships to break down. The higher up a dancer gets, the greater the risk, and the replacements are literally waiting in the wings or in the back of the theater. When your usefulness wanes, the terrible truth you always knew jumps out from the corner: SURPRISE! You are not considered an artist! Not a painter but paint. Not a sculptor but clay. Not the dance but the dancer.

You are an art supply.

Some dancers are recognized as artists eventually. But even they may reach the day when they are no longer useful to choreographers and directors in the same way. Hopefully, they can transition into a position where they finally do have influence as artists, and ideally they have been recognized for the unique artistry they brought to the work of other people when they were performing. Reaching that kind of height is rare and precious. Consider Wendy Whelan, a queen of my ballet age, and her story told in the documentary *Restless Creature*. I do not know her, but I could feel in the film that even after her fabulous, well-recognized career, she struggled over what to do next. She arguably reached the greatest height for which a ballet dancer can hope, and she still wondered what she had accomplished and whether it was worth the sacrifices she made. Most hopefuls are picked off by injury, cruelty, or nature long before the summit is even reached.

Dancer: "I love ballet!"

Me: "Ballet called. It does not love you back."

HAMSTRUNG

Oh, I didn't believe to see you
So quickly extinct, O flowers;
You have passed away like love
That only one day lasted
Perhaps new life
my tears will bring to you,
But to revive love
My tears, oh no, cannot

Vincenzo Bellini
"Ah! Non Credea Mirarti" from *La Sonnambula*
Translation by Elise Curran

After the dress rehearsal and accident, I drove my carpool buddy, Sean, home and then went to my little apartment. He became a welcome conversation partner during that dreadful month of December and the many months that followed. In a

sea of selfish, shallow thinkers, Sean was able to be a bit deeper
and, as a man, didn't have to deal with any feelings of competition or comparison with me. I ate a snack and iced my bruised
shin and foot. The next day, my back began to ache during class
and the performance. At first it was just part of the post-car-
wreck feeling I had in my whole body, soreness and tenderness
in all the bruised areas of my legs, feet, and arms.

On Sunday morning, another show day, I blinked awake
before the alarm went off. I loved my little twin-sized bed, a
comfortable space all my own. A few months prior, Drew and I
had walked about eight blocks with it from her apartment to
mine. Our world was one of shared objects, clothes, experiences, and spaces, but the little bed was mine and in my own
room. Pictures of Brendan, ticket stubs, and fairy drawings
covered my walls. But that Sunday, as I tried to roll over and
snuggle down for a few more minutes of peace, a searing, debil-
itating pain seized my lower back.

My vision whited out for a moment as the nerve pain shot
up my spine and down through my glutes. I tried to sit up,
could not, and rolled myself onto the floor. I army crawled bit
by bit out my door and down the hall to knock on the sliding
doors that opened into Kari's room. The new berber carpet we
were so glad to squeeze out of our landlord was scraping
against my forearms and left them itchy and raw. I told Kari I
was afraid something was really wrong. My back was spasming;
the pain was terrible.

That day I became *La Sonnambula,* the sleepwalker. In one
of Balanchine's famous, haunting ballets, a lovely dancer comes
out in her sleep and dances her way into a poet's heart, but she
is aware of nothing. The poet is in love, but an unjust circumstance leads to his death. *La Sonnambula* cannot do anything
but mourn. I never danced it, but I saw it on video when I was
young and have watched it on YouTube many times since then.
The analogy between my life and the ballet's story definitely
breaks down; it's not a match. But any time I see a woman in

crisis solemnly floating through her difficult circumstances, disassociating, I think of a sleepwalker. When I look back at my young self, I see how I sleepwalked. And why not say it in beautiful, sonorous Italian, like in a ballet? *La Sonnambula.*

Not an anxious girl, I had never imagined things unfolding this way. Life inside my head had always been great. At least, life inside my head *when I imagined the future* had always been great. The great hope I had in a dancing future buoyed me through whatever murky or choppy water I encountered. Now the choppy water capsized my plans. There was no grid for my present reality, so I had to check out. I retreated to a new kind of little world inside, a little classroom, a laboratory in which I tried to puzzle over what might happen next. But like in a bad dream, the most frightening, vulnerable moments stand out with alarming detail, while the mundane weeks and days blur together into a gray, sad smear. I wish I could remember it better, but it's difficult to recall a season I actively fought to forget even as it engulfed me.

Every movement I made was a challenge. I could hardly walk, shower, or dress myself, but I fully intended to go take the warm-up class on stage and dance my roles for the day. I'd done it before. Adrenaline and determination had carried me through so many classes and performances on bleeding toes, tendonitis, even a stress fracture in my foot.

There would be two performances since it was a Sunday. Getting into my car, a low-slung, green Dodge Avenger, was my first hurdle. Stooping to bend into the driver's seat caused my back to spasm again. When I got settled, I moved my scarf from my neck and tied it tightly around my waist and hips to see if that would help. I can remember the deep, pulling, burning pain and the feeling of tiny gasps and muted shrieks pressing from the inside against my clenched teeth. Eventually I learned the liturgy of back injury, how to move through each part of the day with intention and care.

At Sean's house, I greeted him with, "My back is wrecked,"

and we drove to the parking garage of the Seattle Convention Center. Up in the dressing room, I suffered to put on my leotard and tights. I breathed in through my nose to help me swallow the audible groans, to not let them out of my mouth. It was kind of like fake-smoking a cigarette when you don't want people to know that you cannot actually handle what is happening. You breathe in and swallow, but you don't let the smoke down in to burn your lungs.

I knew this new problem must be from the fall. What else could it have been? But I behaved like denial was a sure cure for back pain.

I was back in my senior year *Nutcracker* with a 104-degree fever. I was back in New York for the summer with cellulitis. Why now? Why after all the promise I felt just a few days prior was I finding myself hamstrung yet again? The business was a bitch, but this seemed absurd, impossible. All the signs were pointing to ballet being my destiny, and yet I believed God let me fall. He told me so as I fell. I had heard, "I'm letting you fall." And now I was badly injured.

In the class on stage, I could not turn my feet out without excruciating pain, let alone do a full *port de bras* in even the first few combinations. Mr. Halby noticed that something was up, and I explained that my back was hurting, possibly from my fall. I only recall his concerned nodding and advice to be careful and ice afterward.

In general, the adult responses were underwhelming. I downplayed the degree of pain I was suffering, and with the exception of the tongue-clicking, frowning physical therapists, no one pushed to find out how I really was doing. Leaping of any kind was miserable, so I was forced to confess to the Ballet Mistress, Anne, that I couldn't do Snow or Company Flowers for a week or so. The Ballet Master or Mistress is like an artistic assistant to the directors. She taught us our parts, and after three years, Anne had some affection for me. Calculations had to be constantly crunched. Which is more damaging to my career? Dancing poorly, asking for a show off, or risking further injury? Anne was kind enough to keep asking me if and when I was ready to get back to the harder roles. I so wanted to say "Yes," and eventually I said it too soon. I really should not have been dancing at all.

I wish I could tell you what exactly my injury was. I got confusing, conflicting information, and I should have had some kind of advocate to help me figure it out. The sports medicine doctor that the ballet recommended told me I had a bulged disc at L5-S1, and other doctors throughout the next months agreed. The MRI and x-rays also showed a deformed vertebrae, and there was disagreement over whether this was congenital or evidence of a compression fracture. Whether my vertebrae was involved or not, my symptoms and films did indicate that spinal injury had occurred. There was an acute injury to that disc. And I danced with it through the rest of the *Nutcracker* run. The orthopedist who was on Team Compression Fracture told me I could have wound up with bone fragments in my spinal column.

Meanwhile, another dancer had the flu. The Artistic Director called her mother *on the phone*. She called the mother and reassured her that the ballet would take care of her daughter. The dancer reported it to us like it was overkill on the Artistic Director's part.

I didn't let on, but it was a punch to the stomach. I thought, "Murphey pulled a piece of scenery right out from under me and sent me slamming into the ground, but no one called my parents. Really?? What am I doing wrong!?" Of course, I felt I knew what I'd done wrong: I wasn't as important. I wasn't as valuable as that dancer.

Every performance hurt my heart and my body. Christopher Stowell of Oregon Ballet Theater at the time, whom I should have been trying to impress, taught company class on stage about a week into my new life with back injury. I sucked. I hurt. I left early. I knew then, walking away from the stage, hearing the applause as everyone clapped at the end of class, that my career was officially in jeopardy.

UNMERRY CHRISTMAS

He's all alone up there
Locked away inside
Never says a word
Hope he hasn't died.

"Jack's Obsession" from *The Nightmare Before Christmas*

Around the time I inherited Drew's bed, Kari bought Stayce's couch, and I loved it. Years later I laughed to discover that it's the same couch in the apartment for the movie *Reality Bites*. I didn't know that yet, but lying on it one early December day, I was definitely sensing that reality indeed bites. The pain was constant and unbearable. I tried to alternate heat and ice as I'd been told to do, but getting up to switch the modalities hurt so much it wasn't worth it. There was no one to take care of me, and I sulked. My thoughts were such a jumble of fear, denial, and oppressive optimism that I was too frozen to even turn on the TV. Every time I'd start to panic, my inner, boot-strap-yanking Texan would start saying, "Now don't go there, girl. It's going to be just fine." I wanted to punch that voice even while hoping it was right.

My roommate Kari and her boyfriend Erik were buzzing with holiday cheer, eager to spend the day together searching for a Christmas tree. I was pissed. I couldn't do anything fun like decorate or shop. I couldn't really even stand up straight, and I tried to prepare myself for the pain of trying to dance the next day. I'm not sure what instigated it (aside from the very obvious), but I snapped at Kari. She asked if I minded moving for them to get in with the tree and supplies later. My hot mess of a body taking up the living room would not fit with decorating. She seemed oblivious to my plight, and she certainly wasn't offering to help me with ice or heating pads. "Kari, I'm freaking out! I'm afraid something is seriously wrong with me and have no idea what I'm going to do! I'm also not going to have enough money to buy gifts or do anything fun anytime soon! Sorry if I don't feel like being all happy, happy Christmas tree!"

Kari made her initial Kari-face of "What did you just say to me?" But quickly she softened, and I saw my biting reality occur to her. "OK, Meadow. It's OK. We'll give you some space." Erik gave me a fist bump, and they retreated to her bedroom while I cried into the back of the peach, jacquard couch. I had never yelled at Kari before. In fact, I had hardly ever yelled at anyone. With ballet threatened, I was coming unhinged. Insecurity and fear, things I'd lorded over using confidence and fantasies of the future, swelled up from my heart and into my brain.

I felt so terrible. I wanted them to stay with me, but I also felt so ashamed for being a downer. I'd ruined their fun day they had planned, and I was glad for their sake that they could go. All I wanted was for her to sit next to me and let me cry in her lap. But I didn't ask. I was unaccustomed to needing people, and I did not like it. Comfort and security had always come from dancing and independence. A few days later, I found a cashier's check for $100 in my room. Kari and Erik were trying to help, but they never revealed that it was from them.

The pain, a zinging, cramping, burning combination of nerve pain, muscle spasming, and vice-grip tightness pushes all other memories from those days to the margins. Preparing food was difficult. Getting in and out of my car was torturous. Driving myself to physical therapy multiple times a week in between check-ins at the theater and half-danced, mostly faked ballet classes became depressingly monotonous. Christmas lights, holiday music, peppermint mochas all were lost on me, *La Sonnambula*. I floated with a burning awareness of the wounds in my back sizzling a hole through every other image.

Through it all, I felt loneliness more intensely than ever before. I was cut off from my friends by my injury, a cage. The lock tightly closed between my L5 and S1 vertebrae. Walking to grab coffee before a theater call, everyone joked and did *saut de chat* over the crosswalk. Not me. I tried to put one foot in front of the other without setting off a spasm.

One early dinner in the 4:30 p.m. Seattle darkness, we sat at a big table we collaged together in the Westlake Center food court. I could almost see the bars of my cage, or maybe it was more like the thick glass that separates the gorillas from a zoo visitor. Christmas shoppers swirled around us. Stressed out parents grasped at wild children's hands to keep them from being separated. My friends laughed and talked loudly. We were always, always laughing or having some short-lived, melodramatic conflict. Normally, I'd be right in the thick of it, but this time I was trapped on the outside by my throbbing, aching prison. Nothing felt funny to me, and I felt angry with everyone for being able to enjoy the moment. With every wave of anger and swell of hurt, feelings of guilt, longing, sadness, and terror overwhelmed me. I was hurt and mad because no one seemed to care, and then I felt guilt for being a judgmental downer. Terror was the only reasonable response in the face of the freight train of pain coming to crash my dreams.

The ballet world could be cold and cruel, but our dancing together kept us warm. A lotus eater who had stopped consuming, the spell was broken for me. This fantasyland we lived in, a constant summer camp of doing what we loved best, enjoying applause, dreaming big about our future fame, and powering effortlessly through late nights of fun and days and nights on stage began to fade away from me. Suffering revealed the more concrete world of disappointments and limitations.

I kept all these feelings and worries to myself. I did not reach out, and no one made much effort to reach in. I remember being honest with Sean on our drives back and forth. He acknowledged the shittiness of it all but mostly just listened, like a good friend should. Brendan and I had been dating for eighteen months by then, but I hardly ever saw him during the holidays. The *Nutcracker* schedule was so demanding, but I cried at his family's house a few times. I felt safe enough there to cry from the pain of my spasms.

In my ballet world, I kept those tears in. I cannot remember what Sarah and Nathan or my other church friends said during that *Nutcracker* season. The doctors and physical therapists spoke honestly with me about how I should be listening to my body, being careful, but I had every reason *not* to do that from my nineteen-year-old, this-is-my-make-or-break-it-year perspective. Beyond when she spoke to me right after the accident, the Artistic Director didn't check in again. Teachers from the school asked how my back was feeling, and you can bet money I said, "It's hurting, but I'm doing lots of ice and physical therapy." No one ever said, "Are you really doing OK?" For sure no one said, "How's your heart? Are you handling this alright?" I would have lied even if they did. I knew I was an art supply, and dried up paint tubes land in the trash.

Finally, *Nutcracker* ended. It did not occur to me to pause and soak in my last show. I was so eager to be done and go home to rest for a week. I was still operating on the assumption that I would get well. After a dozen years of dancing in *The Nutcracker*, it was suddenly over forever, that last show passing by me unacknowledged. Christmas would never be the same as before, and neither would I.

DYING SWAN

And who would want to dance with you...
Tell me that it's nobody's fault
Nobody's fault
But my own

Beck
"Nobody's Fault But My Own" from *Mutations*

Writing in my journal every day became essential:

> I'm very afraid of auditioning because I'm just not dancing
> well (my back hurts). The idea of quitting is becoming a very
> realistic option. It's a lot to swallow. My mom described it as
> being so close to the edge of our seats that we've fallen off and
> are shocked to suddenly be on the ground.

Auditions the year prior felt like my own personal self-
esteem booster. I didn't need a job yet, but I was regularly told,

"If you decide you're ready, give us a call." Or, "I'd love to have you, but of course Artistic Director has first pick." Before the accident, I was dancing better than ever, but now? I lurked in the back of classes and continued to fake my way through. If I knew no one was watching, I marked the steps or just didn't do them at all. I made sure to put myself in the authority's face for everything I knew I could do pain-free (or at least pain-manageable) so that they wouldn't get too suspicious.

After one particularly upsetting audition class with a visiting director, I asked to see the School Director. I sat in her office and gathered myself to say, "I need more help. I would love to have some referrals or mentions or some kind of assurance that you can explain my situation to these people who are coming to look at us. Last year, that director loved me. Maybe you all could just explain that I was injured in that accident and...."

"Stop," she interrupted. "You have to stop going back to that."

I was stunned. *"Going back?"* I thought. *"I'm not going back. It's right now."*

"You need to start thinking more positively."

I wish I remember the rest of her words and what I said. I walked out thinking, "These people don't get it." She gave me the sense that this was on me. There was no understanding that I had been truly damaged. I'd never been anything but cheerful and hard-working. Why would they turn on me like this? I wasn't whining. I was still doing my best to be useful. I thought I had earned some help, kept up my end of the deal, but apparently I had not. I still feel baffled by that day in her office. Was she covering company ass? Was she serious? Did these people think my spinal injury was the result of negative thinking?

There were no options left to me at PNB. PDs had to fly or die once their time was up, and mine was up. I had to find a new place to dance. I sent out my audition packets to companies. They contained a nice letter, a resume, and beautiful photographs of me dancing.

I got a call from one company, Carolina Ballet. I spoke on the phone with an assistant or ballet mistress, and the invitation was made: "We'd love to have you come and audition. Mr. Weiss plans to hire new dancers this season." I made a plan with my parents for my dad to meet me in Raleigh-Durham. I hoped that I could fake things well enough to get hired. My crazy flexi-legs still worked; maybe they would want those. I could still turn. Maybe I'd be able to crack off a few great pirouettes and fake them out enough to get hired. It wasn't that I wanted them to acquire damaged goods. I truly hoped I would heal. I believed I just suffered bad timing, and the injury would resolve. So I packed up all my prescription anti-inflammatories and got on a plane bound for Raleigh.

Good thing my dad met me in North Carolina, because I was a wreck. This was my last shot at fulfilling my dreams of becoming a ballet dancer, but I was in pain and not even sure I wanted the job. Getting a job in North Carolina meant leaving Seattle, my church, my friends, and Brendan. It would have meant starting all over. I did not have the energy to start a new soap opera in a new state with a new ballet company and a boyfriend on the other side of the country. But I had to know if I was "good enough" to be a professional dancer. So I went to the studios and took a class, and I danced OK. I knocked out quadruple pirouettes, but I felt mediocre otherwise.

I heard, "Mr. Weiss asked me to tell you that you're a beautiful dancer, but we have no contracts left for this season."

My heart deflated. I could not tell whether they were truthful or not. I did not know how to console myself. I was upset that I would not be a dancer, and it was time to face the fact that leaving Seattle to dance would have been better than leaving Seattle to not. Mom had already been hinting at their preference. "Maybe you just need to come home," she'd say. I would dodge it.

Driving back to our hotel, my dad didn't say anything, but my thoughts were a storm. I had worked my whole life toward becoming a dancer, and now my dream turned to water in my hands, something I could no longer hold. I wondered whether it was my fault, if I just wasn't talented enough, if I was somehow using my injury to excuse my insufficiency. And now I had to face the possibilities of going home, of having my new favorite human become my long-distance boyfriend. The thought of Seattle slipping through my fingers crushed me flat.

I felt abandoned by my art and my own body. For years, when people would ask me about myself I would say, "I'm a ballet dancer." I would wake up every morning and go to ballet class. I exercised all the time. I created art every day. The ballet half of me was going to leave. It felt like my closest friend had a terminal illness.

My parents would not be able to support me in Seattle without the money from my scholarships and stipend at the ballet school. I would have to go back to my prairie and study at Amarillo College. How would I tell my friends at home who expected good news? What would the Hesses say? There would never be a picture of me on the studio wall. With that thought, I began to cry. I fell asleep crying; I woke to cry in the night; I cried through my shower the next morning.

On the plane back to Seattle, my own inner monologue failed me. I did not have the words to encourage myself, to say it would be alright. My eyes burned from weeping the night before, and the lump in my throat was constantly throbbing.

I took a shuttle from the airport to my apartment. The weather in Seattle was cold, windy, and wet, just like it had been in North Carolina—as if both cities were told to make me feel unwelcome. I feared the bitterness that was sneaking into my heart.

My only choice, I decided, was to make myself be positive, to "keep on the sunny side." Everyone liked sunny Jessica the best anyway. When people asked how I was, I would say "fine."

I wanted to just keep my head down through the two lame-duck months I had left. I was not being myself anymore. *La Sonnambula* plastered a creepy smile to her face. I did not feel fine, and I wanted to scream every time I was in the ballet studio. I had to live through it, suck every last bit of ballet out of my life that I could get. I could not figure out a way to give my emotions release without feeling unthankful and bitter.

My opportunity to let it all go came at the 2002 Green Lake Presbyterian Easter Eve service at which people could share publicly about their lives. I stood up, choked on my sorrow, and tried my best to convince myself aloud that my troubles were teaching me to trust God more and therefore were worth it. It was all I knew I could say.

Pastor took my hand and said, "Jessica, the best thing you can do right now is mourn your loss and let Jesus handle your pain for you." I was relieved but also embarrassed. His words rang true. I knew I was fighting to keep grief at bay, and it was not working. I needed those words he said, but they also left me feeling like grief was just one more thing I couldn't do right.

Still I needed him to give me permission to be sad. Having spent my life constantly evaluating how grown-ups were feeling and striving to keep anyone with authority happy with me, I struggled over what to do with all these negative, displeasing emotions. I could no longer please the dance world. I think that night I was trying to convince my new church family that I had a good, right perspective on God as much as I was trying to convince myself that there was a point to my tragedy.

My budding belief that God was worth following hadn't yet grown into a belief that God really loved me. I thought I had to be perfect for him. I tried to apply the answers I had learned to questions about God.

Q: What do I do with the bad things that happen?
A: Remember he intends all things for my good!
Q: Was God aware of what was happening?

A: He controls everything that happens; *not a hair can fall from my head without the will of my Father in heaven!*

Q: What do I do with these tears?

A: Rejoice in suffering!

Q: What if I can't keep it together?

A: I can do all things through him who gives me strength!

I was missing the element of his grace. Grace is God's ability to know who we are, love us, and treat us as though failure had never come along. I thought sadness was the same as thanklessness and ignorance of God's providence. I understood basic ideas about God, but I didn't know him very well. When Pastor answered me with encouragement to be sad and even to offer my messy feelings to God, he introduced me to a new version of God.

Things were only getting sadder. God got bigger just in time.

* * *

A few weeks later, I was in the Artistic Director's office, and she said, "I'm sure the University of Washington would love to have you in the dance department." That for me was the true death knell. She may as well have said, "Correct. No one wants you, so maybe go convalesce somewhere else." I may have considered applying to the University of Washington dance department, but I was in so much pain everyday. I suppose it's inconsistent for me to have thought I could fake my way into a ballet company somewhere (deluding myself that I would heal) while also knowing that I wouldn't be able to dance for a college. I needed time for the whole, terrible truth to dawn on me: I wouldn't just be unable to dance for a professional ballet company. I wouldn't be able to dance at all. Back then, ballet education was not very diverse. We were given token lessons in other genres but not enough.

I might have considered returning to Mr. Hess and Lone

Star Ballet and trying to recover there, but in a bizarre turn of events, Mr. and Mrs. Hess were being drummed out of town. I still do not fully understand what happened there, but somehow Mr. Hess's competitors, people he had mentored and trusted, found a way to get him fired. It was something about using university funds for the Lone Star Ballet. If I had flown back in 2002, I would have been an injured birdie coming to a disheveled, abandoned nest.

Five months had passed since the accident. I saw a doctor once a month or more. I was dancing at 50 or 60 percent of my prior capacity, and the pain persisted. I went to physical therapy outside the ballet twice a week and tried to get in with the ballet's PTs every day if I could. To see PNB's therapists, I had to put my name on the schedule in parentheses to the side. I needed lots of medication and PT to survive the pain, but any company member could come along, cross me off the list, and put her name there instead. It didn't matter what she needed or how badly she did (or didn't) need it. Benefits were for people with contracts, and I did not have one.

Back during our *Nutcracker* carpooling, Sean had given me a CD to borrow, Death Cab for Cutie's *We Have the Facts and We're Voting Yes*. I just let it play and play for six months. I didn't know about signs of depression yet, about how losing interest in things you once loved (like obsessively lining up your indie albums for every possible car ride) might indicate the creep of depression. That music soothed me, though. It was the perfect mellow, wistful, melancholy soundtrack to my gray-cloaked pilgrimages to the clinic as I slowly realized that ballet was no longer a career option for me.

THE ELECTION

My able body isn't what it used to be

Death Cab for Cutie
"Title Track" from *We Have The Facts and We're Voting Yes*

During those last couple months at PNB, I invented a way to stab for PNB success. Stayce and I decided that we deserved some credit for all the advocating and representing we did for the class, so we invented a Professional Division Presidential Election and began campaigning. The whole thing was in no small way an attempt to have some kind of high school experience. I'd missed out on all that as a homeschooler. We exacted endorsements from teachers and staff, made posters, and did a stump tour. Opponents stepped up, and the race was on. My fervor to win my made-up election was pretty maniacal, but I kept it under control. Crazy on the inside, poise and humor on the outside.

Someone had planned a big, Cinco-de-Mayo-themed party

for the PDs with May birthdays, Stayce included. We decided to hold the election there. Stayce and I began the night with her visiting mom and a dinner at the top of the Space Needle. We got dressed up, and I loved my shiny blue pinstriped, very tight, button-up dress. I brought a gift for Stayce, a little jewelry box engraved with the words: *Act I, Scene I, ~finis~*. Inside the box was a beautiful letter from my heart about how I was certain God had put us together for this Professional Division scene of our lives for a reason. I was so grateful for her. She and I had been partners in crime and co-comedians. She gave good advice, found everything funny, and gave me an appreciation for scatological humor that has only grown with time (and been essential to my being a half-decent mother). On our way to the party, I was sure we would win our election. We were the dream team that class needed!

Guess what—we lost.

Of course we did, we were out-going students, and a pair of first-years who would be around the next year took the race. My friends, all the people moving on to careers, all the future primas, used the election as an opportunity to write vulgar things on ballots and be derisive. Yes, it was just a silly thing. Yes, it was ridiculous how much I cared about it.

I went home from the party to an empty apartment and sobbed. I thought, *Why can't I just have this one thing?* I sat in the uncomfortable, red-vinyl kitchen chair and cried loudly until I was exhausted.

I had heard a story from Pastor about a time he felt miserably low and prayed that God would comfort him. He reached his hand out and felt the touch of another's, though he was alone in the room. I kept my head down on the kitchen table and prayed: "Just give me the touch of your hand on mine." The request was a lyric from a song Nathan had retuned. He had recently debuted the song at church, and it had been stuck in my head all day. I tentatively lifted my hand into the air and squeezed the last burning tears down my cheeks.

I felt

nothing.

I looked up at my empty kitchen and realized how uncomfortable I felt in my tight dress, how my black eyeliner was all over the table and my hands. *"Pathetic,"* I thought. *"I am absolutely pathetic. What did I expect? It's not like being the president would have saved my back or my career. No wonder God's not here to comfort you. You did this to yourself."* I was still just a four-year-old ashamed of running circles around the coffee table.

No glory or redemption to be found in made-up school elections, I refocused my energy on enjoying and surviving my last six weeks as a PD. I also started chatting up the PNBS administrative staff to see if they could give me an office job. I wanted to do everything I could to find a way to stay in Seattle. Coffee jobs and retail were out of the question because I could not stand up for more than five minutes before the pain became unbearable. Dancing was a little easier than standing still, but I was no longer good at it.

One day, the School Director came and found me, led me by the hand to her office, and pointed to her computer monitor. Dave, the Summer Course Resident Director, had emailed her to say that he'd love to interview me for a counselor position. I rejoiced! That job would buy me three summer months in Seattle, more time to make a long-term plan.

FINAL PERFORMANCE

My body is a cage that keeps me
From dancing with the one I love
But my mind holds the key

Arcade Fire
"My Body is a Cage" from *Neon Bible*

The final company ballet for the year would be *The Sleeping Beauty*. When I was a little girl, my mom and dad would sometimes let me rent a movie at Video Warehouse, and I always chose Disney's *Sleeping Beauty*. I would flit about as a young, young thing and hold Tchaikovsky's themes in my head and heart. One day, the Royal Ballet's *Sleeping Beauty* was shown on PBS, and my mind was blown. "You mean this is a BALLET?!?! You mean that music is BALLET music!?" I was deliriously happy! The choreography I saw on the screen gelled in my head before I even knew I was trying to learn it. Mr. Hess once scolded a group of us for singing the Disney lyrics to the waltz. "Don't do that!" he said, and I never did again.

My dramatic heart loved the scenes with Carabosse casting her curses and Aurora's death-throes dance around the stage, but who did I love the most? The fairies. So many fairies, all with adorable choreography and music. If there was any part of that little girl that didn't want to be a ballerina, it gave in completely upon sight of *Sleeping Beauty*. A few years later, at Summer Intensives around the country, I learned lots of solos from the ballet, and I still know them all. I especially loved the giant *envelopes* for Bluebird.

The first ballet I was cast in as a Professional Division student was *The Sleeping Beauty*. It was the first time PNB would present the work; Ronald Hynd and Annette Page came from England to stage it. They had both been dancers in the Royal Ballet. Of course, that first run I had very small bit parts, but I got to be on stage while that wonderful music played and add my little smile and body to the scenes. It was heaven.

I was the baby Aurora's wet nurse, a role explained to me by Ms. Page as she bounced and squeezed her huge, imaginary milk-makers. I found it embarrassing, but who cares?! I would be on stage for all the fairies' variations. I loved every minute. I also learned the part of nymph, a baby fairy in the *corps de ballet*. I laid on stage as a sleeping noble woman while the awaited kiss was planted, and I sometimes harassed the Prince with a rubber snake in the much-coveted, flattering role of Hag #1.

Three years later, I was struggling to make it through what I understood to be my final weeks as a ballet dancer. A better dancer than my first year, even injured, I was cast to learn and perform more respectable roles than wet nurse and hag. I was learning Lilac Fairy Attendant—a tutu and wing wearing part that I loved. I would dance through the whole, beautiful prologue with all those fairies. But one terrible day at my doctor's office, he let me know that my back was clearly not healing fast and that, yes, that pain was dangerous. I divulged that dancing Lilac Attendant was hurting me. We agreed that it was probably a better long-term decision to let it go.

I had to go to Anne the Ballet Mistress and again confess that I couldn't hang. I was afraid that I'd hurt myself even worse or make too many mistakes because of pain.

I kick myself for that decision now. I don't know that there was an alternative, but I wish I had just pushed myself to do it anyway. At the time, I made the decision to protect the show from my potential poor performance and myself from being removed from the part. Instead of dancing my way through my favorite ballet scene of all time for my last performance, I stood on stage as a member of the court in a hideous gown and wig. I was a sunken ship and watched everyone else dance everything I had ever wanted. I hated every moment and would silently cry through the whole thing. I didn't even try to hide the tears pouring from my eyes, but of course, no one ever noticed because no one was watching me.

* * *

I planned to take it easy through *Sleeping Beauty*, so I could save what pain tolerance I had left for the School Performance. Each year, the Professional Division students had our own showcase at the end of the season, like a school recital. I had good parts. Stayce and I were cast as opposites, part of a little trio with a kid named Graham in *Divertimento No. 15*, a Balanchine ballet. I loved it, and I even got to *develope a la seconde* on my best side. I also had a part in a tango ballet choreographed by one of the company members. I enjoyed both parts and was eager to dance them for Brendan, my mom, and my sister who would be visiting from Amarillo.

The final days rolled around, and the misery of *The Sleeping Beauty* fell behind me. One day Stayce and I sat under the barres after class, and she said, "You know, you're handling all this so well. You're strong. I wouldn't be able to be so calm."

I was surprised and honored. "Well, I don't have much choice. I don't think freaking out would make it feel any better. And it is awful. But it helps that I believe God has some plan for me."

"You don't seem like it's awful. You're handling it better than you think."

"Thanks."

A few months earlier, when Kari was diagnosed with a stress fracture in her metatarsal, Erik had given me a similar little speech. "Meadow, you're strong, girl. Kari has this thing happen, and she's falling apart, all a mess. But you've got this much worse thing, and you still seem to have a handle on everything." I was so glad he noticed. It was hard to watch Kari freak out, tough to keep being kind and empathetic. She was dancing in the company, and I was watching the entire world of dance ride off into the sunset without me.

I was proud of my composure, but I also knew that it was largely due to denial and shock. The rest can be credited to that desperate grasp for meaning. I tried to just be thankful for the small things that went right and the very big relief that I didn't have to leave Seattle quite yet. School Performance would be as great a finish as I could wish for, and I'd deal with whatever came next.

* * *

For performance day we would have our very last class together on the stage like a company. The day before was our dress rehearsal day. My mother and sister were on the plane, and I was having my final class in the studios with my beloved Professional Division. The company gone for summer, we were in Studio C, the biggest and most beautiful. It all felt pretty grown up. Mr. Halby taught the class, and we were all dancing with joy. When it came time for *grand allegro*, we didn't really want it to end, me especially.

I do not remember what else the combination contained, but it was long and ended with a *cabriole* and a sweeping run off the "stage." I'm not sure why it was there or if anyone had tried to fix it that morning, but we all were aware of a slick area downstage left. In my joy and sadness, in my desire to feel my dancing body just a bit longer, I danced the combination an extra time and found myself doing that last *cabriole* on the slick spot. I heard the pop, landed badly, and crumpled to the floor with a shout of pain.

I lost it. For the first time since I'd cried in the dressing room the day of the *Nutcracker* accident, I could not keep myself composed inside the walls of the Pacific Northwest Ballet. I let myself scream and cry but not too loud; it was the only fit I ever threw there. Mr. Halby came over and said, "Is it bad, dear?"

I sucked in my bottom lip and nodded "yes." And then I shouted at him, "Haven't I had enough shit happen to me already!?"

"Ya," he said, his face falling for me. "Ya, you have, dear. You have."

The sprain was severe. Even if I had decided to suffer through the pain, my ankle would not have mechanically functioned. Stanko Milov, one of the star principal dancers at the time, carried me to his car and took me to the doctor. Stanko asked the doctor if he could just give me a shot to get me through this last important show, and the doctor and I both looked at him with pity. "No," said the doc. "This foot isn't going to work for a few weeks at least."

Back at the studio, my understudy for the tango ballet reportedly uttered a "Yes!" when she was told she would be dancing an extra part in the performance the next day. Stayce got in her face about it. "It's messed up to be happy about something bad happening to someone else!" I appreciated Stayce's offense on my behalf and the fact that she spoke up, but I didn't even care anymore.

A friend drove me to the airport to meet my mom and sister who were in the air while all this happened. I met them at baggage claim hobbling on crutches. *La Sonnambula* became a corpse; I wasn't sleepwalking anymore; I was dead, a ghost. There was no composure, only confused sobs or an eerie quiet inside me for the next twenty-four hours.

Back at my apartment, I laid on the couch while my mother and sister cleaned my room for me and moved furniture. It's a Meador strategy—when in doubt, clean it out! Here I was again, helpless and miserable, struggling even to get ice for myself. The next day, mom felt she just couldn't come to the show if I wasn't in it, and I understood. I didn't want to go either, but I wanted to be with my friends.

In the dressing room, Stayce cried more than I did. Everyone hugged me over and over again, and I was back inside the glass cage. I could see it all, and I loved being there for them and for me. But I was separated from them with a finality that still clangs in my ears. I watched the show from backstage in a daze. My tears had dried, and I couldn't believe that everything had happened so fast. I'd done the spacing rehearsal just two days prior, and now I stood there in tiny, beautiful black pants, a gauzy teal top, and a stylish walking cast.

When my ballet with Stayce was about to begin, I was surprised to hear Stage Manager's voice over the microphone, "In today's performance of *Divertimento No. 15*, Jessica Meador will be replaced by Angela Napier." Stayce and Angela stood together in the wing with Graham. That's when I wept, and School Director walked over to me and clamped her arm around my shoulders as I shuddered through the entire ballet. I accepted it as comfort, but part of me wondered if it was just nicer than clamping that hand over my mouth. During the final bow, Stayce ran into the wings and dragged me onto the stage. My friends clapped for me and handed me a big, beautiful bouquet. I wished I could disappear. I didn't want for it to be happening, didn't want it to be real.

We took lots of group photos and everyone was teary. But then as everyone else changed into dresses for dinners out with their families and met flowers and crowds at the stage door, I slipped past easily. I painfully limped the two blocks home in my giant boot; my ankle had swollen as I stood backstage for so long, and the familiar throb in my low-back refused to show mercy. I felt more alone than ever before.

HOSPITAL ROOM

Baby don't worry cause now I got your back
And every time you feel like crying
I'm gonna try and make you laugh...

Bright Eyes
"Bowl of Oranges" from *Lifted, or The Story is in the Soil, Keep*
Your Ear to the Ground

At the end of my lonely limp home, more disappointment waited in my apartment. My mom planned to take Erik, Kari, Brendan, my sister and me out to dinner, but Brendan had called to say that he was too sick to come. He struggled with rounds of what later was labeled Cyclical Vomiting Syndrome (CVS). I wanted so badly to see him; I had wanted *so badly* to walk out to him from that stage door. We did our dinner without him, and it felt like a funeral.

Before I went to bed that night, my mom sat me down with a talk in mind. The gist was that she thought I needed to reconsider being so committed to Brendan. She thought we should ease up and that I should see other people. All this sounded awful to me. She said, finally, "Do you really want to be with someone who might always be sick when you really need him most?" I hated that she said it, but it did feel like a real question I needed to consider.

In the morning, Sunday, Brendan got much worse, and his doctor admitted him to the hospital while I attended church with Mom and Whitney and then drove them to the airport. I would miss them, but I was relieved to be alone. My head and heart were swirling with the events of the last few days. Sitting quietly in a hospital room sounded attractive.

The Riberas, Brendan's parents, were glad to see me and offered their sympathies for my miserable weekend. I felt so sorry for them and understood what a stress and burden Brendan's mystery illness must be. Later on in the night, they both went home to have dinner and be with the two little brothers. I stayed with Brendan. I sat on the chair in the corner with my ankle elevated and watched him rest. He looked terrible and groaned with pain even in his sleep. Sometimes he'd wake up to vomit. Every now and then a nurse would come in to refresh the stack of emesis basins on his tray.

Did I? Did I want to be with someone who was sick like this? CVS was no joke. How would I answer?

It seemed so terrible to say, "No. I'm nineteen, and I don't want to sign up for someone else's problems." But, I was *only* nineteen, and we were very exclusive. We'd been talking about marriage since month four! Was it foolishness? Was it naive and immature to think that I'd found The One? Was I playing at grown-up too soon by deciding to be with him forever, better or worse, sickness or health? He hadn't asked me to marry him or anything. Not yet. But it was definitely what we wanted.

Brendan rolled over suddenly and made the terrible, strained screech of someone who just has nothing left to throw up. He spat the little bit of bile into the pink emesis basin. I walked over, and he met my eyes as I said, "I'm so sorry, honey." He closed his eyes and dropped his head sideways back into sleep. I sat back down, lifted my ankle back up.

No nurse came for a while, so I got up and grabbed the basin to rinse it out at the sink. I looked down at my boot, and my thoughts flashed on everything I was losing. I had no choice, and I knew the loss would change me forever. Brendan had no choice either; we didn't know for sure, but maybe his forever was changing too. I stepped off the lever that ran the faucet, and looked back over my shoulder at him. I decided right then that I didn't want anyone else to ever be in the position I was in right then. I felt special to be there with him in his misery. I wanted the job, and I'd lost enough already. Besides, I loved him.

.

DISCIPLINE

Here it is the revenge to the tune
"You're no good,
You're no good you're no good you're no good"
Can't you tell that it's well understood

Elliot Smith
"Waltz #2" from *XO*

In those first months of surviving the blow I had been dealt, I tried to staunch the bleeding by telling myself, "It's all part of God's plan." And an entire Greek chorus around me was ready to support that notion at every turn.

These are real things people said to me:

"Maybe God knew dancing would make you arrogant, and so he took it away."

"God obviously wants something else from you."

"That may be a lifestyle God didn't want you to have. Maybe you would be tempted to sin, and he is protecting you."

Before people began preemptively explaining to me *why* God was "doing this," I was not wondering why. I already believed he was good and in charge. I knew he could have kept me from falling, healed my back, and restored me to the ballet life I loved if he wanted to. I also knew that he did not appear to be doing those things. But I was not upset with him. I was discouraged, grieved, but never angry with God or afraid he might not love me.

But when people said, "It must be because [fill in the blank]," I received the message that maybe I should be wondering more about "why." As a dancer I was accustomed to assuming that anything and everything could be wrong with me and need correction. I always took every piece of feedback, considered it, and applied it. But I began taking it pretty hard. I was already feeling down and alone, and after all the "encouragement," I also started to think that my tragedy meant God was unhappy with me.

I did not get very much palpable empathy, but I got a lot of instructions. That surprised me. My Green Lake Presbyterian Church family had, so far, embodied the love of God in a life-changing way. I expected deep, insightful help and companionship in my time of pain. Of course instruction can be helpful too, but the way people approached me made me feel like they just needed to make sure my theological ducks were in a row. I felt unseen and misunderstood. I wasn't railing against or questioning God; I was just heartbroken.

* * *

In times of suffering, Christians have some go-to phrases and passages used to pacify the one in pain. Throughout my life, I became familiar with the often trite though usually true "Band-Aids" offered to me at arm's length. Phrases like "everything happens for a reason" and "when God closes a door, he opens a window" get distributed regularly (My sister-in-law points out that this last phrase is particularly irksome as it's not from Scripture but just *The Sound of Music*. I knew I liked her.).

Like most children, I loved Band-Aids. They make it look like the giver is doing something helpful. If the wound is small enough, the Band-Aids keep the blood under control and the ugly scab out of sight. But at twenty years old, the spiritual Band-Aids didn't cut it anymore. Circumstance reached into my body and snapped the neck of the dancer who animated me. She was paralyzed. Still there, but paralyzed. Her love, her thoughts, her feelings filled me up, but she could no longer move our body. Band-Aids do not cover paralysis.

I thought it was my fault that people did not understand. Maybe I hadn't explained it very well. My dancing wasn't a lark. I wasn't doing some after-school activity. It was a career. I was a teenager already embarked on *a career,* a life in the fine arts. But, more than a career, it was an identity. I was a dancer who could no longer dance.

I was afraid to use a dramatic example, but everyone understood what a big deal it was when Nancy Kerrigan was assaulted. I knew I wasn't an Olympian on TV, but I identified more with her story than I did with the stories people told me about missing the varsity football team *by that much. People don't see me like a Nancy Kerrigan. That has to be it,* I thought. *They can't see the place in my lower back that burns like fire and aches like a never-ending charley horse. They don't know I need more than Band-Aids. Will my church, my friends mourn with me if I can't be a dancer, the person I've been my whole life?* I expected that surely Christian triage had levels beyond "Band-Aid." It does, but I didn't seem to get bumped up.

Sadly, I think most of us have a very poor theology of suffering. Christians may cover their awkwardness around pain and loss with Bible verses that are easy to remember and say; it gives us something to do, and doing is easier than being. I needed people to be with me. And there were definitely things they could *do,* things like help me carry groceries, refill my ice pack, or bring me french fries. But when I talked with people, they had Band-Aids.

At one dining room table, a man opened his Bible to the book of Hebrews and read these words from chapter twelve:

> *My son, do not regard lightly the discipline of the Lord, nor be weary when reproved by him. For the Lord disciplines the one he loves, and chastises every son whom he receives." It is for discipline that you have to endure. God is treating you as sons. For what son is there whom his father does not discipline?*

I waited for him to keep reading, to get to the part that would apply to me. I knew the verses he was reading, but I didn't understand what they had to do with my current grief. He looked up and said, "God does these things to people he loves. When you have hard things you have to endure, it means God loves you."

I was baffled. I wrinkled my brow. "So, you think this is God's discipline for me?"

"Well in a way all the things in our lives are God's discipline for us."

"Huh. OK."

Not much else was said. I wanted to latch onto this offering of his. I knew then and now still that he intended to comfort me. Was this next-level? Was this an Ace bandage, some kind of gauze wrapping, something bigger than a Band-Aid? To be told that my tender pain was God's discipline for me did not feel healing but instead stung violently. And more than the word "discipline," the word "chastise" was hard to hear. I was very familiar with discipline. I was a ballet dancer, for goodness' sake. To me, "discipline" meant limits. It meant denial of everything that doesn't help reach the goal. If God indeed was taking ballet out of my life as a discipline, then I had some serious reflection to do. I presumed that the discomfort this man's words caused indicated a problem with me. *Clearly*, I thought,

I'm just way worse than I knew, and I've completely misunderstood who God made me to be.

I walked away from that conversation and many others like it thinking, *God has done this to me to change me. He's taking ballet away, so it must be something I'm not supposed to have.* After all, I had asked God all the time to make me who he really wanted me to be. I asked Him to shape my circumstances, to make himself the most important thing in my life, to make me long for his will above all else. I had been on a spiritual mission to be single-minded.

A lie was planted deep in my heart, a lie that said, "You were selfish and delusional to see yourself as an artist." The Christians were saying stuff that confirmed the lie, and the ballet world had dismissed me with hardly a bat of the eye. Based on what I could see and hear, I was alone in thinking my ballet self was my real self, a whole, good person. From that sad, lonely place, it was not a huge leap to conclude that the lie was true: no one, not even God, wanted my dancing.

INTERMEZZO

OFF STAGE

If I could get ready for an attack of longing for dance, I would, but all I can do is react once it comes. The attacks come out of nowhere and with very little predictability, though the triggers tend to make sense in hindsight.

They might occur in the shower when I catch sight of my own long, flexible calf muscle as I bend down to pick up something. I might spot the Space Needle from the freeway and mentally walk from the landmark, past the amusement park, around the huge fountain, to the back door of the bright, modern Pacific Northwest Ballet School. I might get a big whiff of Aquanet in line at the grocery store. Hazel Belle might ask me to put on *Swan Lake* for her to dance. Anthropologie may be playing the *Nutcracker Divertissement* during the holidays. Brendan could have a Stravinsky record playing when I come out for breakfast. A PNB poster starring a former classmate wearing a sparkling tiara may suddenly appear in every window on my block. Neil Young might sing "I wanna see you dance again," and then Brendan and I both will cry.

No matter the push, the fall is the same. I suck air quickly through my nose to keep my heart from coming into my mouth.

My limbs tingle with the need to stretch and flow. I open up my shoulders and spread my clavicle wide. I close my eyes and audibly sigh. The first thought is always, *Oh, I miss it so badly.* Then I am officially undone for the day.

I have a few go-to methods for handling these icy, nostalgic waves. The first is to dance, but I only do that when I am alone. I find a mirror and make beautiful poses for myself with my upper body. I might walk back and forth through my house with dancer steps, peeling my feet slowly off the floor, articulating my lower legs like fern fronds unfurling in a time-lapse video. I think my feet will always point, but I have to check to see how much lower my *develope a la seconde* has dropped. Then I get sad. If there's time and the tears come easily, I let them. If I'm too frozen to cry, I Google songs that I know will crack me open.

In public, I stutter or stuff, depending on the company. Brendan will listen to my garbled thoughts, my regrets, my shock; so will my best girlfriends, but I almost never tell them. With anyone else, I generally stuff the feelings no matter how forcibly they have knocked me off course for the day.

When sleep doesn't cure me and I wake up the next day still thinking about dancing, I have to make a plan. The first few years the plans were elaborate schedules for retraining. The initial step was always to take a ballet class. About half the time, I'd go through with it. Then I would spend days in pain and depression afterward. I finally learned not to do that.

Now, the better plans are for me to draw or write. But sometimes I clean all the bathrooms and try to stop thinking about ballet instead.

PART III

THE FIRST SUMMER

Cruel to say
I've known the best of my life
never again to hear
the river's song so clear

Sunny Day Real Estate
"The Ocean" from *The Rising Tide*

I have a light-gray down comforter that has a delicate pattern of slightly darker fern-like leaves. It is getting clumpy, the way down-stuffed items get when you are bad at laundry like me. I love it. It's made for a twin size bed, so I don't get to snuggle under it much anymore. I pull it out for the kids' beds from time to time. I can tell that it was probably expensive, but I didn't pay a dime. I claimed it from the mountain of orphaned items left behind at the Sigma Kappa house following my summer as a counselor for the PNB Summer Intensive.

The sorority house the ballet rented had a lots-ofmattresses, dorm kind of smell. It had one fancy section of white carpet and couches. A large crystal chandelier hung in the center of a spiral staircase. The dining room had carpeting and floor-to-ceiling windows with long curtains that retained food smells, so even though Kermit, the cook, was excellent at his job and fed us quality meals, the room always smelled of stale tater tots. The house was two buildings pasted together with hallways and staircases, and I remember it taking me a while to completely learn my way around. We used an intercom system and walkie-talkies to communicate.

"We" were the dorm staff, charged with looking after about two hundred middle-school and high-school students who came to Seattle for the summer to dance and learn at PNBS. By the time the final group was checking in to the dorms, they could feel very proud knowing that thousands of girls and boys had tried for a spot that summer. It was a great feeling that I missed terribly. Participating as a counselor on the wrong side of the check-in table left me feeling everything but proud. Only about a month had passed since I was the one in a black leotard and pink tights, and my ankle had barely recovered from the sprain I suffered in my last class. My back was still miserably painful and would remain so for several years.

I was thankful, though. I'm really not sure *why* exactly they hired me to be a dorm counselor. There is a part of me that theorizes they were trying to keep me close and relatively happy so I would not try to sue them. After all, I had been injured in a stage accident. Over the years, I have chosen to believe that they just really liked me for being the happy-go-lucky, responsible Elise that I was. I'm sure they knew I would do a great job at whatever role I was given, and that's what I did. Regardless of their reasoning, I was thrilled to have the position even though it was mind-bendingly difficult for me.

A few days before the students arrived, the counselors moved into the house to clean, organize, and learn the ropes. We also needed time to get to know one another and gel as a team. There were five girls: three current University of Washington students and two former dancers, myself included.

These were the early days of me deciding how to act post-injury. In every new situation, with every new person I met, I had a choice to make. Do I talk about dancing or not? How am I supposed to present myself? It felt dishonest, incomplete to not introduce myself as a ballet dancer. But because I was very suddenly no longer a dancer, it also felt dishonest to try to identify as one. The only way to feel like I was being myself, something very important to me, was to share the whole story, to be that weird person who honestly answers the question "How are you?" when asked. Seated around the long rectangular table in the dining room, meeting each other for the first time, I wrestled with how to introduce myself as I waited for my turn.

I had to tell the truth about what had happened to me because I wanted people to know I was a dancer, but it felt icky at the same time. It felt like an over-share. I felt people didn't really care or want to know. But I wasn't sure how to be without being a dancer. I had always considered ballet to be THE special thing about me. My dancer status had been my go-to ice-breaker, ego-booster, core identity for almost my whole life. Being stripped of it left me floundering.

I barely heard a word the other counselors said about themselves, and at my turn I said:

My name is Jessica Meador, and I was a dancer at PNB until just a few weeks ago. I'm really excited to be a counselor because I definitely know what the kids will be going through, and getting this job is what allowed me to stay a part of the whole PNB world even though I'm not dancing anymore. I was injured during *The Nutcracker*, and apparently I'm not going to be dancing professionally like I had planned. So, I may lose it at some point. It's really weird to be doing this behind-the-scenes kind of job when what I really wanted and was JUST doing was being on the other side of it all. So. Yeah. I'm Jessica.

Dave, my new boss, very kindly made some transitional comment on my behalf like "Yeah, this will be a change for you, but I'm sure the kids will be glad to have your help. Glad to have you on the team! Next we have...." Everyone else at the table had looks on their faces that said everything from "Oh, poor thing" to "Damn... she crazy," but no one used any words.

I did lose it a few times that summer, but only when alone. My little counselor dorm room provided the solitude for crying and journaling. It was a small, monastic room in a peak of the roof. Usually, my tears would be set off by something hard happening to one of the students. A boy broke his foot during the first week or two of the five-week course, and I cried a lot for him. I can see now that I was crying for myself too. I welled with compassion for the lonely, scared, intimidated girls.

One girl put highlights in her hair with some of her friends. When the mother was told, she was so angry at her still-beautiful daughter that she called to have the counseling staff arrange an emergency, corrective-color appointment that cost hundreds of dollars. I felt especially sad with that girl. I recognized her tears. They were drops of pure terror, the sure conviction that she could lose love. She just wanted to play with her friends.

I hid my shame in my room and suffered the lashings of my sense of failure. I was embarrassed that I had (been) dropped out of the ranks. I remember how little respect I received from the older dancers, the ones hoping to be given the very spot I had just left within PNBS. They would have treated me very, very differently if I had been in the studio in my leotard and tights. I would have been assigned value. But as a non-dancing human, I didn't carry much weight in the world I had occupied the last three years.

* * *

Halfway through the course, I decided to take an "Open" ballet class at PNBS, one for anyone from the community to take. I went to the studios with all the students, and I didn't know where I should change. My locker belonged to someone else. I couldn't make it through the class, and I didn't even know what problem to blame. There were too many choices: the ankle, the back, the heart, the brain. I gathered my things to get out and was keeping the emotions in check, but everything came spluttering out when Mr. Halby crossed me in the hallway and asked how I was.

"I just can't do it. It hurts way too much," I said.

"Well, it's too soon, dear. You haven't had enough time to heal," he replied.

"Yeah," I said, but what I thought was, *"You don't get it! I'm not just injured. I am ruined. I don't just mean that my back or my ankle hurts. I mean that it hurts my soul. It hurts my whole ME to be in that room and try to be someone I love and don't get to be ever again."*

My eyes filled with tears, and I blinked them at Mr. Halby. He reached out and cradled my cheek and chin, gently rattled my head, and said, "It'll be OK, dear." He clapped the other hand against my waist a couple of times and then spun me like a *pas de deux* partner to send me down the hall.

I went to change and thought, *"Easy for you to say."*

I tried to fill my days with fun. I tried to make new friends in my fellow counselors and succeeded. We had a great time eating ice cream bars and whatever else we wanted from the kitchen. We jello-wrestled in a baby pool just because we could. We spent our days on the sunny lawn in the pool while I tried not to think of the dancers in class. At night we found fresh ways to tease the guard and watched movies on the big-screen TV. I behaved like this was all fabulous, and it was. It was a great distraction for me, but it was a pretty messed-up way to spend my first non-dancing summer of my life.

One of the other counselors, Jessie, was my favorite. We had a blast together and were constantly laughing. One day while we were joking around, she said, "I'm so glad you turned out to be so fun. I thought you were going to be so weird! That first day when you talked about being a dancer I was like, 'OK, she's a crazy ballerina. Probably going to be weird having her around....' But it turns out you're cool!"

At the time, I took her statement well. I took it to mean what she intended, that I was cool and fun to be around. I was glad to hear that! I always prided myself on being a fun friend, and I was very happy that I still had that going for me after losing so much else. But now I see another angle, another message I absorbed, "You being a dancer is weird for me and inaccessible. You struggling through the greatest loss of your life is unpalatable." Whether I processed it that way at the time, I don't know. I do remember registering some hurt later that night in my bed as I mulled over the moment. Sadly, her comments confirmed my suspicions and fear that what happened to me was not a big deal to anyone but me, and the quicker I could become something different, the better.

I didn't have to be different for Brendan. I felt like I had to be fine for my parents because they were devastated for me and still might insist that I move home, though I moaned to them anyway. People at my church had no clue what I had lost, and trying to explain it to them just left me feeling like an idiot, a whiner, or a theological ignoramus. Pam Nolte was different, though. She was an actress for Taproot Theater married to Scott, the director. She openly wept after service one day as I told her my career was over. I remember recognizing the truth and appropriateness of her tears, and I wished I could let myself be as sad as she was.

Another noteworthy exception to the general Pollyanna attitude was my mother. Mom knows sorrow, and she was able to feel the depth of my loss much more acutely than I at the time. She didn't glibly say that everything was God's plan. She didn't try to cheer me up. She used the right amount of reminders that God is good and loving. But since she also wanted me to come home (of course she did; how could she not?) I wanted her to think I was OK.

In heavy times, my dad's comfort usually came in the form of a strong, quiet, affectionate presence, like it had in North Carolina when he just let me lie on the hotel bed and cry as he stroked my hair. But I was far away from him now and words over the phone were not the same.

Brendan was able to sit with my sadness and listen to me go on and on about how nobody got it. He cried with me, and he told me he loved me. I knew that to ever leave our relationship would be to lose someone who had seen my heart like no one else. I had my complaints about him. I could see the ways our differences would create friction in the future. I love demonstration, huge gestures, and he doesn't seem to need a thing. I can read the emotional nuances in a crowd, and Brendan might not see a thing. If he does see it, he'd prefer to leave it be. But I wanted to stay with him regardless. We had already endured Cyclical Vomiting Syndrome, career loss, and terrible physical pain together. It was an investment neither of us wanted to leave on the table.

DESK JOB

Cheer up, honey, I hope you can
There is something wrong with me
My mind is filled with radio cures
Electronic surgical words

Wilco
"Radio Cure" from *Yankee Hotel Foxtrot*

My drawing became precise and wildly creative at the same time.
I spent hours sitting on the floor with my knees up, chin tucked
on top, and arms wrapped around to draw at the coffee table in
Kari's and my little apartment. I outlined lively, intricate, impossible scenes from nature: big whales in fields of corn, suns rising
with stars from caves full of bats, wax hearts melting in fires and
dripping down into one mold of a giant heart. I painted or filled
the drawings with colored pencil. To me they were elaborate
doodles just meant to fill the time, but when I recently found a
stash of them in a box of old photos and letters I cried over their

bright beauty. I filled with compassion for the broken twenty-year-old woman who didn't know she was doing art therapy.

I spent a lot of time alone. Summer was rough, but at least it had been sunny. As the school year began, there was nothing to protect me from the bleakness of my first year without ballet in my life. Actually, it was worse: ballet was still in my life, but I was no longer in the ballet.

* * *

During the Summer Course, I was periodically given a day off. I loved the opportunity to sleep in my own bed for a night. The morning I rose to visit North Seattle Community College, I was in a good mood. Even though NSCC couldn't stand up to NYU or any of the colleges that had accepted me during high school, becoming a college kid held attraction for me. I could wear my hair down and my underwear the entire day! Not having to wear tights everyday is the only perk to being a non-dancer that I've ever seen.

It was time to go to college. If ballet was out of the picture, I needed a real job. On the return drive across the Aurora bridge, with the community college application on my passenger seat, I cranked up my radio and felt some of the freedom I had enjoyed in high school when driving to WTAMU. KEXP, Seattle's indie station, was playing a new band, The Postal Service, and I was excited to hear Ben Gibbard doing something different as he sang, "...the stranger with the door key explaining that I'm just visiting."

I was on my way to interview for a job behind the desk in the PNBS office. I would have no reason to go down the hallway once there, no reason to yank open my locker and strip down, no reason to saunter into the studio and lay myself down like a starfish in the light coming through the window. A stranger with the door key, I could still get in and was still known, but the ballet would never again be a home to me. I was uninvited from the space I had most longed to occupy my entire life, the studio.

Instead I was offered a position as an administrative assistant. Being an Elise had benefits just as I expected. The ballet had noticed my non-dancing skills. I was personable and positive. I would sit in the school office, enter data, answer the phones, and field questions. I would be on first-name basis with all my former teachers and directors. Halby insisted that I call him Fleming, which felt good.

I knew it would be torture to sit there, to hear the piano music waft in to taunt me rather than animate me. It paid well, though, and my body could do it. I could make more money than I would at a coffee shop, and I'd be able to afford rent and groceries. I could then use some funds sent by my parents to pay tuition at NSCC. I would not be dancing, but at least I wasn't leaving Seattle! I felt I had failed my childhood self by not becoming a dancer and lost my first great love, but was glad to have a ticket to keep Seattle and Brendan. The price was the pain of staying so close to the ballet.

* * *

After a few months in the office, I realized I had access to my files and could look up old audition notes. My coworkers goaded me, and I finally dug up the note from my Summer Course audition as a thirteen-year-old. The pencil markings scratched on a piece of yellow, legal pad paper read:

ft., t.o., ext. <u>*WEIRD*</u>.

I knew the translation: "Good Feet, Nice Turn Out, Notable Extension. Weird." There is a reason dancers are willing to say all kinds of harsh things about themselves; it starts with the people in charge. I probably was a weird, excited dancer from a small town school at thirteen, and we all laughed pretty hard over it. Honestly, though, I'm not sure what to make of it, and I still worry about being "weird."

I did not find nearly as much information as there should have been regarding my injury and my last year. Every time a fax or email came in from a doctor's office or physical therapist, we would make a copy and staple it into the dancer's file. Every dancer had a detailed file. I can only guess, but I think part of my file was locked up. Or there was no record because they didn't really keep one. I do not know. Both options are equally upsetting.

* * *

Fall came; the weather turned, and I drooped. I had never felt the common Seattle curse of seasonal depression. I'd always been so consistently high on endorphins, but not anymore.

At first, it felt like a blessing that I could still see my friends everyday. People with whom I had danced were beginning their first and second years as company members, but they all quit calling and visiting pretty quickly. So did I. It hurt too much to see them, and I had great difficulty giving a flying rat's ass about their problems at the ballet, about spots at the barre and casting. Eventually I could hardly be around Kari anymore. I'm not sure she understood or was able to understand; and I wasn't very fun for her either. I'm sure I was a cold shoulder when she needed to vent. Our apartment days came to a swift, discouraging close.

But I loved my little sisters, the girls who had just started in the Professional Division the year prior. They would come find me in the office, confide, and ask me for advice. Lauren Zelt was my very, very favorite. I saw an opportunity. I could help protect and support the students. I could make sure they had the medical attention they needed. I could make them feel safe and be a listening ear. I could soothe and encourage them. They could tell me anything, and I would never betray their trust, never mentally mark them off the list of desirables. I made it my mission to watch out for their well-being. I was twenty years old and trying to make lemonade. I revived the role from Hess School of Dance days: Protector.

* * *

My schedule was filled with full-time coursework and twenty-eight hours a week of work. Sometimes if things in the office were slow, I could sneak a little homework on my office computer. I didn't fit in with anyone. The college-aged kids at church all went to the University of Washington, like Brendan, so I felt a little second-class as a community college student. My ballet life had no use for me, and I had no time to try to make friends at my school. Christians continued to mostly say hurtful things about God and what he thought of me. The two years I spent at NSCC were hard, cold, and depressing, which matched well with the all-concrete campus. A few good memories stand out, like when my future best friend and I tried to take a cardio hip-hop class, but mostly it sucked.

I don't want to use the word "refugee" flippantly, given the current geopolitical climate, but that is how I felt. My expulsion from the dance world left me muddling through in a new context where my education didn't count, my encyclopedic knowledge of ballet had no use, and my love for dance history was lost on others. The social currency that had taken years to earn lost its value overnight; the norms and customs I enjoyed with dancers were strange and off-putting to others. I was no longer getting hugged and petted everyday.

I was never the loudest, silliest person in the room when I was a dancer; theater kids and dancers are always on a mission to entertain, *especially* each other. But suddenly people at college and at church were always giving me the wide-eyed side-eye or saying things like, "Oh! Oh my! You just say what you think there, don't ya." If I broke into song or all the chore-ography from *West Side Story*, no one joined me anymore.

"Am I OK?" I started asking Brendan after every outing. "Was I being too much or something?"

"I think you're great," he'd say. "You're just being Jesky, and I like you that way." Of course, he also was dating me, so I didn't count him as unbiased.

One bright spot in my confusing new context was Marsha Novak, my physical therapist and Feldenkrais practitioner. Her office was in the funky neighborhood of Fremont, and except for the challenge of parking and making it up the long staircase to her floor, I looked forward to going. The hour consisted of exercises and manual therapy. I couldn't wait to get through the spinal articulations and balance practice to be able to lie on her table and have her magical hands and skill provide relief for my broken body for at least those twenty minutes. She knew the dance world and admired it, but I could speak honestly with her. She could see what I was going through and gave me sympathy and comfort twice a week.

COMPENSATION

All my lies are always wishes
I know I would die if I could come back new

Wilco
"Ashes of American Flags" from *Yankee Hotel Foxtrot*

In spite of the resistance I often felt from the managers at Pacific Northwest Ballet, the state covered my medical expenses. My Labor & Industry claim via worker's compensation was a major stressor. Because I was injured during a rehearsal, the ballet insisted that I should not be covered by worker's comp. Students were only paid for performances and would, the ballet said, only be covered when they were being paid. The smart-as-a-whip office manager at my doctor's office and the AGMA (theater union) representative at the ballet disagreed. The union representative advocated for me, and the office manager submitted the claim. The state accepted it. The headache of all of this added insult to injury and more stress to my final days as a dancer and to the next two years.

To have a claim with the state means to constantly need to prove on paper and on phone calls that your injury is real and that you deserve to receive medical care. I saw two medical examiners, independent doctors who evaluate on behalf of the state and patient whether the claim is legitimate. While I was clearly injured, the state and I disagreed about how great a loss this represented. My case manager told me over the phone, "You can't expect to lose a job as a star baseball player and then find equivalent compensation or employment." I understood that, but I wanted money for retraining. I'd spent my life and my college fund learning to be a ballet dancer, and I needed help to pay for college. The state finally grew tired of paying for physical therapy and sent me to one last, grandaddy-of-them-all examiner to decide what my final compensation should be.

He was quite literally a grandaddy, had to be in his 80s, a guess that I later confirmed. Overwhelmed by it all, I invited a friend from the office, Ellen, to come with me. We found the big downtown building and took the elevator way up to the floor of his clinic. I felt like I was going to see the Wizard and shared Dorothy's hope: "If the Wizard is a wizard who will serve, then I'm sure to have a [favorable outcome on my exam]." I was channeling the lion, too, with a wish for nerve!

In the waiting room as I filled out forms, I suddenly realized which underwear I was wearing. Stayce and I had begun a trend of exchanging THE most ridiculous thongs we could find. Opening night, holidays, birthdays all were marked with the giving of a tiny, rhinestone, shiny, feathered or mesh thong. They all fell to the bottom of my drawer, and I generally knew it was time to do laundry if I had to wear a novelty thong.

There I sat—young, terrified, and convinced that this geriatric doctor would think I was somehow trying to influence his decision! I told Ellen my plight, absolutely hoping she would offer to trade me. "I'd totally give you my underwear, but I'm not wearing any today." Yeesh. Now it's a funny story, but then I was mortified. I was heading into this crucial exam as ass-out as Drew in *Chaconne*.

I went into the exam room, changed into the gown, and tried to keep my naked cheeks covered. I answered the questions the old man asked me, and then he asked me to do various movements. The final check involved him holding open the back of the gown and asking me to repeatedly clench and unclench my glutes. I have no clue whether this was medically necessary or not, and I was alone in the room with him. "Humiliation" gained new depth.

* * *

A few weeks later, my phone rang in the middle of my Intro to Psych class. "I'm so, so sorry!" I said as I rustled my bag to find the phone. Then I saw by the area code that it was probably my L&I case manager calling to let me know what happened with that peep show/exam. "Ack! This is important!" The instructor looked shocked and said, "By all means." But I was already jetting out the classroom door.

"Hello?"

"Yes, Ms. Meador?"

"Yes!"

"Your examiner determined you have a Category 2 impairment."

"OK?"

"Your claim will be closed. Look for the information in the mail."

"OK."

"If you have questions...."

He went on about a new number to call or something, but my head spun. Closed? Category 2 impairment? Do I accept all this? Do I have to? I said "goodbye" and then slunk back into the classroom.

"Well?" said the instructor. "Did you win the lottery?"

"Nope. But I might have lost."

Within a week or so, I got a check in the mail for just over $7000. I'm told they have a chart. One axis has body parts; the other has levels of impairment or maiming. The place where the lines intersect has the amount at which the state will compensate. My spinal injury was worth $7000. At the time, I was thrilled. Every quarter of school, I hoped I'd be able to afford my tuition and books. This money would help buy books and pay the application fees for the University of Washington Foster School of Business where I hoped to transfer.

BACKSTAGE HELPER

Water pouring from her eyes
Alcoholic and very bitter

Elliot Smith
"Baby Britain" from *XO*

As part of my admin assistant job, I worked backstage for the School Performance. The first year, when friends of mine were still dancing, I spent the whole show trying not to cry, but I was doing a terrible job. I wept openly, and Artistic Director said, "Jessica, what are you so upset about?"

"I'm supposed to be on a stage not back here." It was a bold thing to say.

"Oh, change is always hard," she said.

I didn't respond and got up to fix my face and get back to work.

Unwilling to repeat that first bad experience, my twenty-one-year-old self decided to try a different approach the next year. I could not wait to avail myself of all the bubbly wine, snacks, and treats in our green room. Once we were finished running dressing rooms, ferrying classes up to the stage, and dealing with nervous-child vomit and urine accidents, we all relaxed and toasted while the older students did their half of the performance. I had no interest in watching the Professional Division do anything and a thirst to be as clueless as possible, so while the PDs danced, I sat in the green room chugging Prosecco. Unaccustomed to using alcohol rather than enjoying it, I didn't have a gauge on exactly how much I was drinking or how well I would handle it.

When the staff came out for our bow on stage, I could hardly stand up straight. Ellen propped me up, but as soon as the curtain closed, I laid down on the marley to feel the warmth created by the stage lights and enjoy the spins. Unfortunately, the curtain coming down was the fake-out before the encore bow. As the curtain rushed back up, Ellen whispered, "Get up. Get. Up!" I popped up but then got off stage. I think I skipped the miserable photo-op in order to go drink water. After the show, up the road at Ten Mercer, a fancy cocktail place, the School Director bought drinks. I spilled half of my "Pirouette," laughed too loudly, and began to feel the judgy eyes. Brendan drove up to collect me, and then I spent the evening vomiting. Honestly, I still think it was less painful than the year of crying, but the guilt factor was off the charts.

The next morning I walked into church to be immediately greeted by Pastor. "How ya doing?" he asked with a smile.

I cracked into tears, "I got drunk at the ballet's School Performance yesterday. I just didn't want to be there, and now I just feel terrible, and...."

"Oh," he said. "Come here." He folded me into a hug and prayed to God into my ear. He asked God to be kind to me and to comfort me. I expected a speech, a scolding even. Actually, I was so ashamed of myself that I wanted to be in trouble. I wanted to pay for my poor decision. To be greeted with love and reassurance when I felt nothing but need for condemnation changed me. I understood grace with my heart and body rather than just my mind.

WAIT UNTIL I'M BEING NICE

You know it seems the more we talk about it
It only makes it worse to live without it

The Beach Boys
"Wouldn't It Be Nice" from *Pet Sounds*

In 2004 on a Tuesday morning in fall, I saw a rainbow in the sky and had a "today is the day" kind of feeling. Brendan and I were in that phase between talking to my parents about getting married and becoming engaged. It was so hard for me to wait. I knew we were having a date that night, and I just felt like the time had finally come. Then, when I arrived at his apartment that night, Brendan had me kill time while he did math homework. He told me we didn't have time to have a date, but that we did need to drive to his parents' house to get some kind of paperwork. I was crestfallen, but I committed in my heart to not throw a fit (again) about when the heck we could finally pick a wedding date.

After a while, he said, "I feel bad cancelling the date. Let's stop for dinner on our way to my parents' place." I tried to be casual and nice in the car, and I made it halfway through my dinner before a leak sprung in my resolve. "When, Brendan? When can I plan? When can I be sure? I just want something to be settled. I want to know for sure that I'm staying here, and that I made the right decision. Everything else we do will be together, but here I am waiting for you do this unilateral thing of asking!" I wanted something to feel secure, reassured; I wanted to know that my dream of marrying Brendan would come true.

"Just trust me," he said. "It will be soon."

In the car on our drive up the hill, the same drive we did from the Arby's that first night, I melted with shame. "I'm sorry. I didn't want to be this way." We parked in the driveway, and I walked around to hug him and bury my face in the smell of his hoodie. He took my hand and led me through the back gate. Then, in about the same spot he gave me that first tulip, Brendan turned me to sit on the garden bench and pulled a bouquet of red tulips out from under it. As he knelt down in front of me, I realized what was happening, started half-braying-half-squawking, and tried to articulate the words, "No! Wait! Do it when I'm being nice about it!"

He said, "Will you just let me talk?" I can't really remember what he said because all I could think about was kissing him. Mark, the littlest brother got an eyeful, I think. His little face had appeared in the window when I started shrieking. I said, "YES!" Then we went in to have our picture taken.

Back at Brendan's apartment, all our best friends were gathered with ice cream and congratulations. We hung out for a long time, and when the crowd dwindled, Brendan drove me back to my apartment. I wanted to stay up all night and have all the conversations that had hitherto felt presumptuous. Where do you want to live? What kind of wedding should it be? All of those things. I wanted to lie on my couch together and just stare at each other. He, however, needed to go home to finish his math homework. Classic Brendan.

Our August wedding was large but pretty simple. We said our vows at Green Lake Presbyterian and partied at the University of Washington Botanical Gardens. The whole thing was mostly stressful, but Brendan was my pride, joy, and comfort. And now he's mine 'til death do us part.

My back was hurting terribly from all the standing the day required, and we ended the reception earlier than planned so I could leave to sit. But, really, I just was ready to go away and be alone with my husband. All I had wanted was to be 100 percent Brendan Ribera's. I wanted to be his greatest pleasure, biggest responsibility, most precious commitment, and finally I was.

We drove our hand-me-down Toyota Corolla station wagon to our studio apartment in Ballard. Our unit was directly above Pasta Bella. Driving away from the reception in my wedding gown had been fun, but as we pulled up outside, I became terribly self-conscious. I made Brendan sneak ahead to make sure the way was clear. It was only five o'clock in the evening, and I didn't want to be seen going into my marital chamber! We made it safely, and I relaxed. Brendan had set up all our IKEA furniture and put flowers from our wedding in a vase on the kitchen table.

That night we had a late dinner at Pasta Bella, and I felt like I had the best secret in the entire world.

HIDING AND QUITTING

Is it gettin' heavy?
Well, I thought it was already as heavy
As can be

The Flaming Lips
"Waitin' for a Superman" from *The Soft Bulletin*

Later that summer, I couldn't take my job anymore. Being at the ballet was too full of triggers. I probably should have quit after the School Performance drove me to drinking, but I didn't. I thought I would eventually get over it all. I hoped that I'd stop hurting and that maybe I could climb my way up the administrative ladder, but all that denial just made things worse, not better. Being married to Brendan was good for my cash-flow and my sense of security. With my future tied to his, I felt aware enough and brave enough to let PNB go. I no longer needed the job, and I let myself admit that I didn't want it.

The Pacific Northwest Ballet School has two facilities, one

at Seattle Center and one in Bellevue, the suburbs. The Bellevue building, where I worked one of my four days a week, had lots of storage space. Sometimes the theater crew would load things from there to take back to the opera house in Seattle.

One day when I was sitting alone at the desk while my colleague was at lunch, Murphey the Stagehand pulled up and got out of his car. I felt everything from annoyance to sadness to rage around him because of the accident and avoided him, but this time was different. Adrenaline rushed through my body, and my breath caught in my throat. I could not talk to him. I would not fake my way through another convivial, accommodating encounter. I felt that I might scream at him: "DO YOU EVEN KNOW THAT YOU RUINED MY LIFE?!" So before he opened the door I dropped to my knees and crawled under the huge wrap-around desk. Well-hidden, I listened to him enter. "Hello?" he said. I didn't answer, and he went off to do what he came to do.

After I heard him disappear, I emerged. I shook my head and thought, *I'm getting really messed up.* My coworker returned in a few minutes, and I didn't tell her what happened. I did, however, excuse myself to go leave a message with the psychologist who consulted for the ballet school.

I sat in Tracy Jewel's chair in her office, looking out the window at Lake Union. I told my entire story to her, and it felt like the first time anyone had wanted to hear it. "Well, I'm shocked that I didn't already know about this," she said. "I can't believe that they didn't suggest you see me right away when you were injured." Over several appointments, Tracy began to unlock the grief, terror, and anger in my heart. She had me write a letter to PNB with all my scathing indictments and frustrations. I was supposed to pull it out and read through it when I found myself paralyzed by my feelings about it. She also pushed me to leave PNBS. "Maybe one day," she said, "you'll be a successful business woman and the ballet will have to come to you to beg for money." I liked that image not because of the begging but because all I wanted was to still be useful in the ballet world.

I quit that week and sent one very important email to the new Artistic Director. I wanted him to consider creating a mentorship program for the Professional Division students and requested a meeting.

Peter Boal was in his first year as Artistic Director. I had an artist crush on him, a crush I'd had since I was seven years old when he signed my ballet shoe for me. I had loved my classes with him at School of American Ballet my one summer there. It felt very full-circle.

Now I had the chance to cross paths one last time, so I went out on a limb for the sake of all the little dancers I had been protecting. I needed Peter to know what had happened to me. I needed him to hear that I felt I was filling a role that could disappear with me. I worried I was the only person in the office who truly *loved* the students, particularly those in the professional division that everyone knew PNB would not keep. His assistant gave me an appointment, and I was so proud to walk into that office. I had nothing to lose. Peter listened respectfully and with interest. I later received an email to me, the school staff, and Tracy Jewel inviting us to meet to create the mentorship program I had proposed.

On my last day at the office, I wrote a long letter that I posted on the bulletin board about how I would miss everyone. I did not receive the champagne goodbye toast that other employees who were moving on always received. Brendan picked me up, and I remember actually screaming, gurgling snot and tears, all the way home to our little apartment. I no longer had any reason to keep my anger hidden and let go of the leash for the very first time. My heart was full of questions:

"What just happened? Where do I put this? Will I ever get over that place? When will I stop wishing I was a dancer?"

A few weeks later, after I'd finished working there, I met the pertinent PNBS staff, Peter, and Tracy Jewel in the library for our meeting regarding my mentorship program idea. I spoke about how I thought it would be helpful for each professional division student to be assigned to a volunteer staff person or company member who would keep the student's confidence and provide guidance. I mentioned that students needed particular help understanding how to navigate insurance, doctors, and Labors & Industries compensation. The School Director oozed disdain throughout the meeting. At my mention of L&I she snapped, "They aren't supposed to have L&I coverage. I'm still not even sure why you had it!"

I went quiet, disabled by six years of obedience and people-pleasing.

Peter intervened. "I will talk to the union rep and make sure we understand how things should work." Tracy nodded her approval and after the meeting gave me a pat on the back. But I was too intimidated and decided not to help anymore.

Occasionally, I would get emails from Ellen and my other office friends, but we lost touch fairly quickly. That's probably on me. I did not go to see the ballet. In fact, I avoided Mercer Street altogether. My mother had to try several times to get the Pacific Northwest Ballet to take her off their mailing list, and I never updated my alumni information.

GRADUATION

You can drive all night
Looking for the answers in the pouring rain

Cage the Elephant
"Cigarette Daydreams" from *Melophobia*

After four busy, emotionally distressed years, I approached my graduation from the University of Washington. I transferred there from NSCC right after Brendan and I were married. The UW called me an "alternative student," one who commutes to campus. I did not enjoy being alternative. It translates to "weird."

I was tired of weird. Married undergrads aren't common. However I was an *excellent* student, attending on scholarships and grants. I happily graduated magna cum laude from the Business School Honors program.

I'm big on celebrating special occasions. I've always been that way, but my ballet experience sealed it. My parents barely saw me dance once I moved away to Seattle, neither did the Hesses. I always played down every part and performance because I knew the cost of them coming to see me from Texas was a big deal. Of course, that's a huge part of why that last-minute sprained ankle was so devastating! We were robbed of the shared experience of them seeing me perform on a PNB stage.

Because I was so disappointed by missing the chance to celebrate my ballet success with my family, I decided to never let a moment pass by unmarked. In that spirit, I threw a giant graduation party for Brendan on the rooftop of the Hotel Deca in the University district. Our friends all came, and we ate and drank under an unusual, cloudless, starry night. Brendan graduated a quarter before I did, and I figured his party could count for us both. I didn't expect any fuss or visitors for mine. But I did tell my mom a few months before my graduation that I would really like for her to come. I wanted to celebrate with her and mark the occasion. I wanted to be proud of what I had managed following the devastating loss of ballet and some redemption for how terribly her last visit had gone. She understood, and we made plans for her to come for my departmental commencement.

I didn't have the interest or energy to seek a career right after graduation, and thankfully I didn't have to since Brendan was making enough money at a great job to support us both. Instead, I somehow convinced Brendan that we should start trying to get pregnant before I graduated. I think I was afraid to go for a big-shot career just then and figured we could just get on with having children so that by the time they were grown and gone I would still be young enough for career and travel! We got pregnant right away, in the spring of 2007.

I called my parents to say, "I'm pregnant!" Such an added treat! For the first time, I felt that maybe there could be a happy ending to the story of my loss. It had been a bleak four years, but in spite of it, there I was: married, graduating with honors, and pregnant with my future. I was particularly tickled by the fact that I would receive my college diploma while pregnant with our first child, just like my mom had with me twenty-four years earlier.

But things took a turn. While Brendan was away on business in San Francisco, I started bleeding. I left him a panicky, tearful voicemail that to this day he still shudders to remember. The next two weeks were a sickening roller coaster filled with blood work looking fine and bleeding improving to gushes in the middle of my work day at the Foster Business Writing Center. A day or two before my mom was to arrive for my graduation, I went in again for bloodwork. While Mom was on the plane, my midwife called to tell me my pregnancy was over. I greeted my mother at the airport with the news that, once again, it was going to be a very rough weekend.

At that point, I was ready to hide in a ball in my apartment, but I decided I should still walk in the departmental ceremony at UW in spite of the circumstances. I bawled my way through church that morning and passed my teeny, tiny baby in the restroom of my church building. When I have to go in there, I think of the first stall as my little baby's grave. Later that afternoon, armed with pads for the concurrent events, I graduated from the University of Washington. I was grateful for the drapey graduation gown.

At the end, there was no party. My mom took Brendan and me to a nice dinner at St. Clouds in the Madrona neighborhood. My crispy-skinned roasted chicken tasted delicious, but the labor cramped and pained me so badly that we decided to take it to go. I remember lying on my couch while Mom stroked my hair.

* * *

Four years prior to my miscarriage when my mom had come upon my dancer death, something beautiful happened. I decided to stay with Brendan. In a similar fashion, that weekend of my graduation, something lovely came again: I learned the gentleness of God toward mothers. I was more ready than ever before to love him and be loved by him for better or for worse. After my ballet life fell apart, I felt close to God but afraid. I was afraid that if I experienced another shattering loss that I might begin to doubt his goodness. But while I was losing that baby, my greatest source of comfort was knowing that God knew my child. I did not get a great business career, but I never really wanted that anyway. I became a mother the weekend I graduated from Business School.

I was surprised again by the array of responses from my most beloved friends, my church family. One friend, Brenna, was hand in hand with me through blood draws and phone calls, and her presence in my messy pain solidified our relationship. But in other cases there was a befuddling lack of response to my miscarriage about which I was very open. Primarily from older people, I received shaming comments like, "This is why most people don't announce so soon," or dismissive comments like, "You're young. You'll have another one."

Brendan's and my parents were empathetic and soothing. I received special comfort from Christy for whom I regularly babysat. She wrote me a card and brought me her own journal from when she miscarried, so I could read it and not feel alone. One day I showed up for a babysitting shift, and I could not stop crying as we talked. "When does this part go away? When do I stop crying?" She said, "I don't know. I became a mother, and now I cry all the time." She was an important conduit for God's parental love to me at that time.

Remembering my graduation means much, much more to me than just a degree. When I see people in cap and gown, I rejoice for them, and I mourn for my lost child (even more now that I see what beautiful, amazing people my living children are). I sometimes cry for myself over the painful, visceral experience I had. In my graduation picture, I'm smiling a tired smile and shaking the dean's hand. To others, it looks like a regular graduation photo, but I bought it because it is my memorial photo of me during our loss. It's a picture of my graduation to the ranks of parenthood, to the state of loving someone more than I had ever thought possible—not for who he or she is or does for you, but purely for the fact that he or she belongs to you.

BABIES

Losing love is like a window in your heart
Everybody sees you're blown apart
Everybody sees the wind blow

Paul Simon
"Graceland" from *Graceland*

Ezra Wray came the day after my birthday in July 2008. There
were six, long-for-me months between my miscarriage and the
new pregnancy. Carrying Ez changed my body in such a way
that my back didn't hurt as consistently as it had. His birth,
unmedicated, challenging, but healthy, taught me more about
my body, my power, and my endurance than I learned in all my
dancing days.

Now he is moody, deep-thinking, and cursed with the kind
of creativity that just has to force its way out. Whether he is
expected to be quiet, asleep, or doing math homework, he sees

connections. His musings either crack me up or completely blow my mind.

Ivo Clark arrived still snug in his bag of waters in the birthing tub we set up in the living room. Babies born in the caul have long been considered a special blessing. Ivo's birthday was the happiest day of my life. The fun, peace, and anticipation hit record-breaking levels. Brendan and I hit a stride of connection and partnership that made me glad for every choice I ever made in his favor. Introducing Ezra to Ivo revealed to me a new kind of love and joy. They are twenty-two months apart.

Optimism crowns Ivo's little dirty-blonde head, and he reminds me of Elise.

Hazel Belle Marie's due date was December 25th. My mother cried with happiness when we learned a daughter was coming. Ivo was nineteen months old when she came. Hazel Belle received the benefit of having a seasoned mother. I did not fret over her and enjoyed her. But, I became very ill by the time she was one year old. Regretfully her toddler years were so clouded by my illness that I can hardly remember them.

Hazel Belle is, in her words, "a winter baby who can face the cold!" We are trying to make up for the difficult years of my sickness with long snuggle sessions, being girls together, and acknowledging the time we lost.

Bran Raphael came relative to my question: "Will some tragedy always come along to ruin my dreams?" With Bran's life, the answer is "No!" The pregnancy, birth, and infancy provided many opportunities for me to experience and show grace; our whole family indulged in his cozy infancy. I learned to protect and prioritize my time with my children.

He sings the songs, hugs the hugs, and smiles the smiles of a well-loved fourth child. Thankfulness and affection flow from him as easily as toddler fits and demands for the red bowl.

* * *

People say, "If you had a ballet career, you wouldn't have all your wonderful children!"

I always smile and say, "Yeah, I guess so!" But inside, I say, *hmmph.*

It's not that I don't understand the point or that I don't appreciate the gift of my family or recognize the attempt to keep on the sunny side. My problem with that kind of statement is the shallowness of it, the inability to hold two concepts at once. Bad things happen, and God is good. You can be sad and grateful. And I am grateful. I love my kids, and I would pay ANY price to have them. But I didn't have to pay the price of my ballet dream in order to have the family that I have. I don't believe it was some cosmic tit for tat.

This works both ways. Dancers have said to me, "Yeah, but I don't have a family like yours." Of course, that statement has nothing to do with me, but dancers are welcome to be sad that the dance world and the United States are incredibly poor at delivering maternity leave, postpartum care, or work after babies.

I do love to tell my kids that being their mother is the greatest privilege I've ever been given, and finding out about each one of them pleases me more than any acceptance letter, casting, or career ever could. I'm not saying that motherhood is some kind of ultimate life experience or goal, but it has been pretty great for me.

Having children has pushed me to better understand myself because these little barometers all around help me to read the pressure. When I am fearful or self-loathing, it comes out as impatience and unkindness toward the kids and Brendan. I do not tend to act out toward my parents, my friends, or others; I am deeply afraid of disapproval, disdain, and rejection. The ballet and my past have played roles in cementing all those fears, but my young family has begun to loosen my grip on the fear of being shunned. We are tightly wound to each other, and I feel safest with them.

I'm not sure how aware I was at the time, but I definitely made a decision to be a great mother in lieu of being great in other ways. I had planned from a young age how to be a perfect mom, one who was never tired, relaxed and fun, and hosted everything. I was afraid to put energy into the other things that attracted me, mostly artistic endeavors, because of what happened with ballet. All my need for achievement funneled into my expectations for myself as a parent. Even at the start, I knew better than to demand satisfaction and a sense of achievement from my children themselves. Thank God for that! I've known those kids (and the adults they become), so clearly burdened by the pressure to make all their parents' dreams come true. I couldn't do that to my children. Instead I put the pressure on myself to be a dream of a mother, one who would do all I could to empower them to live their own fabulous lives.

Once my children began to hit school age, the giant wound left by my ballet loss became raw and symptomatic. I suspect it manifested as illness, but I'm certain it revealed itself through pathological, damaging, and dysfunctional responses to threat and stress. Parenting is laden with opportunities to fail, to not be perfect, and even though I technically knew I could not be my children's everything, I behaved like I should be. I would tear myself apart for the slightest mistake and even things that were not mistakes, things like needing to buy a ready-made dinner instead of cooking baby food from scratch. Stress and exhaustion set in for a long stay.

I did not know my unresolved issues with the ballet had

anything to do with my daily life. I was unaware of my need for treatment until I was nearly completely disabled.

WISHING FOR DEATH

And in your heart you know it to be true
You know what you gotta do
They all depend on you
And you already know
Yeah, you already know how this will end

DeVotchKa
"How It Ends" from *How It Ends*

In the wee hours of a spring night, I dragged myself back upstairs to my bed after quieting my crying baby Hazel Belle. My heart slammed in my chest, and I realized it was totally arrhythmic. I shook Brendan. "Feel my heart!" Thump, thump... thump. Thumpthumpthumpthump... THUMP. We were alarmed, but mostly we were excited. THIS was the clear, problematic symptom we could take to the endocrinologist I was scheduled to see. It was 2013, ten years after I limped home alone following School Performance.

For months, I assumed I was a lightweight who couldn't handle having three kids under four years old. Chronic exhaustion, pain, dizziness, disturbances to my vision, difficulty breathing, and pounding heartbeat had become a regular part of my existence. I told myself over and over again, "Buck up, lady! They told you motherhood was hard!" But that night of the arrhythmia, I knew for sure something was really wrong.

The endocrinologist's interest perked up as my symptoms displayed in his office. He was administering an orthostatic test in which vital signs are taken in prone, sitting, and standing positions. When I stood, my heart went into tachycardia. It felt like it might motorboat right out of my chest. "It's happening right now," I said. "This is the feeling I get all the time."

"Well, I won't let you fall. Let's just see how this goes."

I moved my head around to keep my vision from totally graying out.

"This could be POTS," he said. "And you don't want that."

Time and further testing proved his suspected diagnosis. It was POTS, and he was right. I didn't and don't want that.

Postural Orthostatic Tachycardia Syndrome, or POTS, is a form of dysfunction of the autonomic nervous system, or ANS. The word "syndrome" is used to define recognized groupings of symptoms that typically don't have one common cause or clear pathology. Without clear cause, one cannot have a clear cure. The best explanation we have for *my* POTS is that a severe flu, my "intense season of childbearing," and possibly my thyroid disease led to an autoimmune response against my ANS. If the body is required to perform something automatically, like adjust heart rate and blood pressure to accommodate postural changes, breathe, dilate pupils, digest food, etc., then the ANS is in charge of it. For people with POTS and other forms of dysautonomia, those automatic functions are no longer a guarantee.

By the time I saw Dr. Davies, my endocrinologist, I could barely function. I had to crawl around my house to keep from fainting upon standing. If I did manage to stand up, I avoided bending down at nearly all cost. Unfortunately, these are terrible restrictions to manage when you have two toddlers and a baby. The dizziness, exhaustion, muscle pain, and digestive dysfunction landed me in bed as often as I could possibly go there.

Before we found the right beta-blocker and other measures to suppress my symptoms, I went downhill fast. I was too sick to watch Hazel Belle eat her first doughnut on her one-year birthday. I couldn't stand up to sing at church. I could not shop for groceries. I couldn't cook or clean. I couldn't pick up Ezra from preschool. I was afraid and depressed. I had told myself my whole life that I wouldn't be a sad, tired mother.

I did not want to live. I was the one who had decided to sign up for Brendan's illness. Why the twist? I couldn't take care of my own children, let alone my house or husband. I had hung my hat on being industrious and useful. I'd left my frou-frou, artsy ways behind. I spent all my time and energy on serving others, and then I couldn't.

I never wanted to kill myself. It wasn't like that. But I did hope that maybe they'd find something else wrong with me that would take me. I told myself that if I died, Brendan and the kids could find a new mommy, someone fresh and strong. I chewed on this dark notion for a few weeks before I finally cried it all to Brendan. He cried too and said, "But Jesky, we don't need what you can or can't do; we just need *you*." It had not occurred to me that I was that worthwhile. Now I feel ashamed that I was selfish enough to only want to do life my way and not another.

When I finally was brave enough to speak my feelings to friends, they reassured me with the same sentiment as Brendan. I didn't doubt my family's or friends' love or willingness to care for me. I just doubted that I was worth the trouble, and I did not want to burden them. I lost my dancer self to injury, and I felt I was losing my mother self to illness. No one had seemed to miss the first me, and I presumed that eventually, when the dust settled, no one would miss this me either.

I began to see a therapist. She, my friends, and my own praying and writing helped me uncover the growth and progress of the cancerous lie. The original lie, "God doesn't want you as dancer, and that part of you was never important," had turned into something deeper, something much worse: "God doesn't really want you, and no part of you is important." I still thought God loved me in a general way, but I operated as though he expected me to earn that love by being useful.

I did not see it all so clearly then. It took a long time of writing and digging to find that root. But because I was a mother, I did have one major "Aha!" right up front.

I already have said that once I saw that God was real, I knew I had to deal with him and had been trying to learn who he really was. God says he is our Father, and often his language is maternal in reference to us because God possesses all good qualities.

If I could see my child thinking that I didn't want her and that no part of her was important, I would be devastated. I would fight to reveal her value to her and say, "NO! No, my love! My darling one, you are as important to me as my own body, as my own deepest dreams!" I would fight the lies to their deaths. The "Good News" truly became good because *that* is exactly what God did, what Jesus did. He fought the lie that we are worth leaving for dead by dying and living for us.

If God loves me the way I love my children, then he loves me half-dead and "useless" in a bed. He loves me as a dancer. He loves me not dancing. He loves me when I doubt his love. He loves me when I'm running from his rules.

He loves me.

He loves me.

He loves me forever.

* * *

POTS changed my life for the worse and better. It's well-managed now. I take a beta-blocker every night. I sometimes swallow giant salt pills. For a while I took Ritalin for energy and to compensate for the cognitive dysfunction resulting from lack of proper blood flow in the brain. I drink Mason jar after mason jar of water, regularly monitor my heart rate, and try to reduce stress. Sometimes I forget I have it, and other times I spend a few days in bed. When it's really bad, I wear compression hose and try not to leave the house so that I will not faint in public. Even on those bad days, I'm so, so grateful it is something I can live with.

If I forget how bad it was, I picture some specific memory like the time I forgot to retrieve Ezra from preschool. I remember the time it took me thirty-five minutes to get up the four flights of stairs at Carkeek Park with a baby and two boys because I kept stopping to put my head between my knees, clutching desperately at the kids to keep them from falling. I think of all the times I crawled around my home the entire day. If I forget to be thankful for how well I feel, I take a good, long look at Bran. His life helped to redeem mine from POTS. But it took awhile to get there.

START-UP

Well I won't back down
No I won't back down
You can stand me up at the gates of hell
But I won't back down
No I'll stand my ground, won't be turned around
And I'll keep this world from draggin' me down

Tom Petty and the Heartbreakers
"I Won't Back Down" from *Full Moon Fever*

Remember analogies on the SAT Verbals? Here's one:
Jessica is to ballet as Brendan is to _____.

1. Cyclical Vomiting Syndrome
2. Push-ups
3. Computer Science
4. Cannoli

While all four things relate to Brendan, the answer is #3, Computer Science.

In the same way that I dreamed of a career in ballet and identified myself with it from a young age, Brendan dreamed of computer programming. He would stay up late making games and doing computer science projects while a towel kept the light from passing under his door. He has a natural talent for logic, languages, and math. People in his life saw his desire and talent and did what they could to facilitate the achievement of his dreams. But when he was at the University of Washington, he tried three times to be admitted to the computer science department, and three times they turned him down. He persisted and took every class he could. He majored in Informatics and minored in Applied Mathematics. He was given a paid internship at a Seattle start-up right out of college, and he has been recruited to better and better jobs ever since. No one yanked any scenery out from under him, and he has thrived in his beloved field. Now sometimes kids from the UW Computer Science School hope they can pass Brendan's interviews.

One aspect of Brendan's computer science dreams was always to have his own start-up. In 2011, he met a potential business partner with a decent idea, and we decided to take the plunge and "bootstrap" it. We helped fund the business by living for one year on all the money we had saved to try to buy a house in Seattle. That meant three more years in our rat-infested rental. A few weeks after we committed, we found out I was pregnant with Hazel Belle. That first year was fun, stressful, frugal, and educational. Brendan and his partner enjoyed pretty regular media buzz and were nominated for Mobile App of the Year at the GeekWire Awards. Apple awarded them "Top Apps" in 2012.

I was so proud of him. I still am. Brendan is talented, humble, easy to love, and grateful. He is all the things I hope I would have been if I had enjoyed career success.

While Brendan birthed PaperKarma, I carried and delivered our fabulous daughter. As we started to consider next steps for the company, I became ill with POTS. The second year was not as fun as the first. Thankfully, two months before I was diagnosed, Brendan's company was acquired, and we finally enjoyed a regular salary and company health insurance. Brendan was the Seattle employee for a Silicon Valley company, and I often think that the only reason we survived POTS before treatment was his flexible schedule.

I was a burden to him. We struggled to understand each other, meet one another's needs, and care for our kids while facing individual Goliaths. In our marriage, we didn't want the other person to have problems that were his or hers alone. We wanted to share, but he couldn't take dysautonomia off my hands any better than I could clear bugs from code and meet deadlines. Foresight of the havoc POTS could wreak on Brendan's career contributed to my swift spiral into depression. I felt that, once again, my body and its malfunctions would smash childhood dreams. That's a huge part of why I was tempted to think my death could be a solution. I wanted Brendan to be free to do what he loved and had mastered.

Of course, Brendan wanted to take care of me and be a consistent presence for our kids, and he did those things admirably. POTS held him back to be sure, but God gifted Brendan with an unnatural ability to survive on very little sleep. He would work and help me by day then stay up late to keep working. We made it through, and within a year we had a new down payment. But an even greater payoff was on its way.

With the appearance of POTS and all our new, big, unwieldy projects, you might think that ballet finally fell off my radar. Instead, I began having flashbacks of pain and loneliness. All the disruption to our plans and dreams, and all the physical pain put me in a kind of continual, PTSD-sense memory of being trapped and afraid. I worried almost constantly that POTS was all my fault, that somehow I had asked for the illness by being so bold as to have three children in three and a half years. Here I was again, I thought, being uppity, thinking I could have a grand life of rich motherhood. I wondered if God was once again trying to tell me to cool it with the aspirations, the delusions of grandeur.

GROWING THINGS

She said, "I've lived my life down under this pile
And it's over my head and I'm so tired
That I want to get out and breathe"

Nathan Partain
"Air" from *People You Meet*

One of my favorite things to do in a new house is to see what kind of plants grow in the yards through the first year. There are always surprises. Although I am a novice, I enjoy gardening and love plants. I like to know what they are all called and a thing or two about them. This is a trait I inherited from my father who still likes to give me a tour of his herb garden when I am home.

At our new house in Northeast Seattle, not many things grew. I did lots of cheerful work to create a cottage garden. Right now, 2019, the flowerbed is spilling over with lavender, peonies, roses, delphinium, calendula, salvia, daisies, poppies, daylilies, honeysuckle, irises, and the blessing of mullein. However, in late spring of 2014, I was tending seedlings. One day, while weeding, I hesitated to pull a little guy growing right by my front steps, a plant I had not planted. It just looked like something special that deserved to live compared to all the oxalis and dandelions being ripped out by the roots. Over the next few weeks the Little Plant That Could got bigger, and I was glad I had left it. I wasn't sure yet whether it was something I should have allowed, but I was still curious and willing to let the little bit of nature take its course.

In spring when the dogwood trees are in bloom I love to celebrate Ivo, who was born on May 12th. It was such a lovely birth, and the beautiful dogwoods remind me of walking the blocks in my old neighborhood with my husband and friend Brenna while I was in labor. In the new yard, I felt sad to be away from our old neighborhood with our sweet, octogenarian, Swedish neighbor and the well-loved dogwoods. I think it was then that I felt my first pangs of regret that none of my babies were born in the house we now "owned."

By the time we settled in the house, my POTS was relatively controlled. I was finally having a break in the shallow end rather than desperately treading shark-infested waters. I had reached a new place in which I felt some hope that I could still have good days, even some great ones!

We were able to take a breath and take stock of things. I had a baby girl who was no longer a baby, a beautiful guest room and master suite that were just begging for a baby, and sons who were wondering when we'd ever have another kid in our family. I could not believe I was thinking this way. My switch just flipped. For a couple of years, being around babies or breastfeeding made me utter a prayer of thanks that I was not expecting, but suddenly my uterus was twitching.... Oh man, I was in trouble.

I love giving birth. Aside from dancing ballet on the stage, nothing has given me the sense of human power and glory but also frailty and dependence like labor and delivery. It is the performance of a lifetime. Therefore I insisted on feeling every last bit of it, every time. I wanted to know what my body could do, what it felt like to be a portal to God's masterpieces, and even what greatly increased pain feels like. I never had any kind of epidural or analgesic during my births. A friend of mine is a nurse midwife, so she cared for me and my babies. Her wisdom and reassurance normalized the idea of home-birth, and I became a true devotee. Pregnancy and birth were the first instances since my eviction from the ballet world that proved the continued value of my body's intuition, my pain tolerance, and my endurance. Not everyone who wants a dreamy, empowering birth gets to have it. I'm very grateful.

I was afraid this little growing idea to labor and deliver another baby of my own was a weed, and I didn't say it aloud to anyone for a while. But I did start asking God to rip it out if it was a weed. I was afraid it was a seed of discontent. Things were feeling so much better. I was basking in my blessings, and here I was wishing for more and starting to be sad that I didn't have—probably couldn't have—another baby.

My endocrinologist had been clear when I began seeing him that he thought I should cool it on the childbearing since reproductive stress is a strain on the thyroid. I was afraid it was just silly and selfish for me to want another kid, and I kept imagining all the doctors (and everyone else) shaking their heads at me and thinking, "Leave well enough alone, lady! You already have THREE!!! You even have two sexes!"

Those anxious thoughts were the true weeds, and they almost choked out the vulnerable plant, the desire to have a fourth child. It took more effort to control those thoughts than it takes to control pesky northwest dandelions. The first time I floated the idea to Brendan, he was definitely surprised but agreed that having another one of these wild, small people would be awesome. We had dreamed of having four children almost as long as we'd been talking about being married.

When I talked to my therapist about it, I walked out feeling for the first time that it was OK for me to have it. I decided to protect it. I prayed about it everyday and watched it grow. I could see that it probably wasn't a weed, but I wasn't sure if it would be OK to keep it forever. I worried I was being selfish. My family already felt unwieldy, and there I was thinking about making it even more so. I'm sad for myself now that these fears were so big, but I'm grateful that they did make their way through my heart and mind. I needed to see how much I still needed to grow in my willingness to just be loved. I decided I wanted to start talking about it with some of our friends and family who would be affected.

While this idea began to grow so big that I had to decide to make room for it, the little plant by my front steps was doing the same thing. I moved a couple other things I'd planted out front because obviously this little guy was meant to be there and loving the spot. I checked it first thing each morning.

In August, just before a group camping trip with friends from Green Lake Pres, the plant made a very interesting little head of buds. It was about to show itself! As we packed the minivan, I decided to share with my friends and brothers and sisters-in-law to get a read on whether my fears had any place. The whole drive there, I ran baby names past Brendan.

On our last day, sitting in the sun on the grass near the beach, I finally broke down and cried and told my friends my precious, crazy idea and how foolish I felt for having it. I was received with love and more tears by people who were willing to encourage me and give me the outright declarations of love and loyalty that I needed to hear. As when I was diagnosed, the trouble lay not with their lack of care but with my struggle to believe that I'm worth any trouble. I was relieved and excited to keep giving harbor to my little growing idea. When we pulled into our driveway after the trip, my plant had bloomed with a beautiful cluster of pink, peachy, precious flowers.

I did a little investigation. It was a Verbena.

I didn't yet know what this new dream was. Was it the first steps toward having someone new in my body and in our lives? Was it the prompting I needed to start saving for an adoption? Or was it the beginning of my need to grieve the loss of my ability to have more babies? I was so scared that the last option was the case that I didn't do the Google search that I knew could answer most of my questions.

Through prayer, I finally arrived at a day when I felt ready to enter the words "POTS pregnancy" into the search bar. Lo and behold, there was a recent study showing that POTS symptoms improved during pregnancy and that it posed no additional risk to mother or baby. Well, that was the boost I needed. I emailed my neurologist who, very kindly, called me to say he thought it was a definite possibility, but that I'd need to see a high-risk OB to make sure things would be OK with my meds.

By the time I saw the OB, I was not nervous. I had read the research on everything and just needed her approval and agreement to all the conclusions I'd come to on my own. It was the very best doctor visit of my life. She was a lovely person, and everything went as well as it possibly could. Compared to the visits I had over the past many years, visits full of fear and confusion, visits where I was told my dreams were dead, the OB visit was such a joy. I knew what I was talking about, and the room was full of hope. She said we could start trying whenever we wanted and that there was "no reason you can't have a baby." She even approved of my home-birth midwife! The beta-blocker I used was already the exactly right choice for a POTS pregnancy.

I had anticipated this would be my moment of truth, that moment when you've ordered the chicken only to suddenly and clearly realize that you wanted the beef. I figured that once all the other barriers were cleared Brendan and I would know whether we really were brave enough, willing and excited enough to accept the reproductive stress. We both immediately reacted with a resounding, "YAYYYY!!!!!"

I was pregnant within a month, and I told people about the pregnancy within days. I knew how it felt to lose a baby and how hard it is to tell them about pregnancy loss. But if they knew then maybe they would remember to pray, and I wanted to enjoy every possible moment of the child's life with us. From the moment the test read "Pregnant," the baby was already bringing me joy and healing.

When we learned he was a boy, I named him Bran because it is the male form of "Brenna," and a "B" name for her and my other besties, Bethany and Blythe. "Bran" is also a reference to Brendan and his Irish half, but I proudly named my son primarily after women. May he embody and exhibit the qualities those great ladies display.

The middle name was tricky. I wanted to use "Raphael." It's a nod to Brendan's and my Italian heritage, but more importantly in Hebrew it means "God has healed me." My POTS was by no means gone, and I didn't want to be presumptuous. I did feel a deep sense of healing though. I felt healed of the fear of being worthless. I chose the name as an acknowledgment that whatever troubles and illnesses I or my family will ever face, we are not worthless. How could anyone God loves be worthless?

The next year, when my garden was filled with blooms and verbena, I gave birth to Bran Raphael. My POTS symptoms abated for nine wonderful months. But even when my symptoms flared up again, I did not despair. I leaned into the joy and love of my family.

THE BALLET CLASS

I am a writer, a writer of fictions.
I am the heart that you call home.

The Decemberists
"Engine Driver" from *Picaresque*

Kay's attic office had the smell of classy perfume wafting in a
library. I crossed the worn rug eager to flop into the old
armchair, drop my shoulders, and exhale as much of the day as
I could. I took time to really look at my therapist and be glad to
have an hour ahead of me to turn over internal stones.

In addition to being a therapist, Kay is a visual artist. The
walls held the strokes of her brush and her eclectic taste; I
always paused to notice what she chose to hang behind the
client chair, to see what she wanted to look at all day. I once
revealed that crows in nature and in old stories, fiction (from my
dreams) and nonfiction (from my life), represented fear to me;
they made me feel like something evil and clever was watching

and waiting to take advantage of me. Kay felt quite differently about them. Before she rehung a crow piece of hers that she loves, she let me know it was coming. Kay's crow, perched on a stack of books and signifying inquisitiveness, didn't scare me.

"Can I start with something?" Kay asked.

"Of course," I smiled.

"I'm reading this book." She held up the thickish, hardcover novel, *The Painted Girls*. There were Degas-styled ballet dancers on the cover. "And it's made me think, 'I should apologize to Jessica.' You know, because I'm an artist, I thought that I understood what it was like for you. I figured I kind of knew how it felt."

"Oh, I think you do know." I paused to quickly scan my memory for anyone who had "gotten it" better. It was on my second session with her that I mentioned how ballet had brought me to Seattle and how I was an EX-dancer. She started drawing out the story pretty quickly.

"Better than most people," I said. "Nobody *really* gets it."

"Well, I was reading this, and just the way they talk about how dancing makes them feel made me think that I really don't know. Dancing seems to be its own thing. Here, if you don't mind, I'll just read this little bit."

I braced myself for impact and tried to relax in the same deep breath.

I wanted to dance as Rosita Mauri did—like a man in fierceness and strength, like a woman in lightness and grace. Afterward she made a low curtsey, and when she looked up, her face was aglow with joy. It was a pleasure I knew, something I had touched once or twice in the practice room, the pleasure of having become music, the pleasure of being filled up head to toe.[1]

"MMmmm. MmHmmm." My eyes roved from the garden-scene painting on the wall behind her, across the neutral wall, landed at the skylight over her chair, and then drifted back down to her as she read.

"Does that sound familiar? 'Being filled up head to toe?'" she asked, looking up at me with curiosity.

With one part of me, I thought, *How lucky am I to have a woman like this try to know me better?* The rest of me struggled to come up with words in response. It had been a long time since I'd been filled up.

"Yes," I decided. "It does."

I played the reel from my mind's eye of the early days. I could see two frames. One contained the audience or mirror's perspective. The other held the view from behind my eyes and prompted visceral memories—squeaking across the floor, breezes stirred up by movements, the damp heat of my body and the studios. Here I was in Canyon, Texas, at WTAMU, though I was only fifteen. I tried to look professional and wear pink tights, but I really wanted to fit in with those cool college kids and wore black tights over my leotard when ballet class was over. Young and raggedly talented. Ebullient. Enthusiastic. Engaged.

Then came memories of PNBS. I never could believe I was good enough to be there. No t-shirts or black tights in the mirror-image now but instead a perfect bun, pink tights, and a flattering black leotard. After a few years' intense training, "weird" had turned to refined. I saw myself having "a good class."

"You had a good class today," Carla, the other girls, and I would say to each other.

"You too! I saw that quadruple pirouette when we were going across the floor!"

"Well, your *saut de chaut*s are INSANE! Your split is ridiculous."

"Well, it was a good class."

"Yeah. I love it when Mr. Kells teaches. I could have done that waltz ten more times."

"Poor Katja! Her hands were getting tired; we all went so many times!"

"I think the pianists just love the drama of making those pained faces." And then we'd laugh and mock Katja's lolling tongue and rolling eyes.

My body sat still in the old chair in Kay's office, but inside I indulged those dancing, happy memories for a moment. Those days were nearly half my lifetime ago. The knot of longing began to form in my chest. I said to Kay:

> I don't know if other kinds of artists understand it or not. But dancing *is* special. To have your whole body so involved is, is, well.... It just fills up your whole self. Like the book said. It's a mind-heart-body thing that I've never duplicated. I keep trying to find it again. I think that's why I love natural childbirth! There's something about the focus required, the demand that your whole body and mind be dedicated to pushing that baby out. You have to give yourself to feeling all the power of it without being drowned by the pain. And there's a purpose. You want that baby. And we wanted to do those performances. To get those contracts, those parts.

Kay gently smiled and nodded.

"This is why I always describe it like a death," I said.

My lower lids filled, and I tried to look up at my hairline and swallow it all back down. This was the right place though. None of these would be things I hadn't said in that room before.

I hadn't come in wanting or needing to talk about it except that I always needed to talk about it; I just had learned that no one else does. I had written the story down a dozen times already: I journaled it all as it happened. I wrote panicky versions of it when I'd hit a new anniversary. I blogged it. I wanted to understand what had happened. The external details were clear; filling out doctors' paperwork developed a skill of distilling the narrative into its most basic parts.

Stagehands made a mistake. I was thrown from the set-piece and fell five feet down onto my hands and knees.

By the next morning, I had extreme pain and spasming in my low back....

Yes, it was clear that I'd never have a ballet career after that injury. My *arabesque* was all but gone, and the pain was never gone. But what happened to that dancer on the inside, in my mind, my heart? I kept writing and writing; new facts emerged every time. I kept waiting to "get over it," "move on." I let myself watch the sad memories next.

I saw myself in black tights and t-shirt, hair pulled back and up but messy, old canvas shoes dyed yellow for *Nutcracker*s past. I was post-ballet, but I had a lot of hope walking back into those studios each time. I wanted it to feel good again. Lying on the rubber floor, feeling the metal *barre* under my hand, pressing my palm down around it, listening to swishing legs and catty secrets passing from snide mouth to eager ear, I started to relax. Watching the rolled eyes and wry chuckle exchanged between instructor and pianist, noticing the familiar press of the floor against the insides of my legs as I stretched, letting my long femurs drop down into the earth, pressing my nose down next to my knee... oh, it felt good. As class began, my body resumed old rhythms and joints cracked back into lifelong demands. I felt calmer with every *plié* and *tendue*. I marveled at my nice legs in the mirror. I tried for one combination to point my feet harder and rotate my legs more. I did my best to crank my *passe retire* to where it "should" be and got a charley horse. But no one noticed. I knew the teacher, but he appeared to no longer know me.

By the time we were moving on through *frappés* to *rond de jambe en lair*, I let myself register the pain getting worse in my lower back. That pain, a parasite on my life, thrived on any attempt to fill myself with dance. The delusion that I could start a slow but strong and incredible comeback evaporated from my heart, mixed with all the has-been sweat, and settled as condensation on the windows of beloved Studio C. Every *grand battement*, even though it was still high by anyone's standards, told me I was a fool. Nothing felt good. Instead of taking a quick break after the *barres* were put away to get a sip of water, I gathered up my things and left. I had done it again. I tried. But I was miserable. Rushing down the front steps, only Dale, the security guard, would ever know that Jessica Meador had been back in to take class.

* * *

Looking up from that sad scene, I wondered why those three or four awful classes take up so much space in my mind. Why does that painful layer so thoroughly muddy my lifetime of healthy dancing? Was it just because it had happened last, like when you overwork a painting and lose those few early strokes that you liked so much? There is no going back. I can never remember the light without it being dragged down by the heavy.

"That's why I pronounced that girl dead," I said out loud.

"The happiness, the music, the rush, and the body are gone. The kick will never be free and high enough. The turns will never sail around and around. The dancer is dead. I remember her; I am her, but without the body of the body-mind-heart combo that is dancing...." I sighed deeply. "That's the loss. I cannot dance. I do not dance. But I'll always, always want to dance. Whatever I can have now is just a gift shop version. I'd rather not have it, so pitiful compared to the real thing."

Kay made a little sound, "Hmmm," nodded more, and smiled consolingly.

We moved onto the more present concerns—my worries for my children, the way ballet fed my demanding perfectionism, the way I pushed through my pain and chronic illness when I should just rest. I had hoped to cry that day. My life belonged to sweet, young people with no control over how much they need from me. I had developed an almost too-good skill of keeping myself together. Days that should have been full of tears were full of swept floors, teacher meetings, and restraint, so I wanted to cry at therapy, to decompress. Starting with ballet was the best thing we could have done.

The next morning, my weeping spilled from my heart and through the open dam so hard to shut. I planned to spend the hours strolling my two-year-old Bran along the paths at Magnuson Park. Miles of trail along the lake, through the wetland ponds, under a rare shining sun awaited us. The baby (as we still called him) loved to look at the geese and ducks. He could name herons and identify the call of the red-winged blackbirds. He couldn't wait to go see the birdies. As we came down the hill from our street and rounded onto the lakefront drive that would take us to the park, the radio DJ played a Decemberists song from my old days, a song that I had liked but never loved. Colin Meloy's confession took on a meaning from my own heart, and I knew I'd never hear it the same again:

> *And I've written pages upon pages*
> *Trying to rid you from my bones,*
> *My bones*
> *My bones*

She isn't dead. She's you. I thought it for the first time. *But you have buried that part of yourself.* That's when I knew that my writing was my digging. I didn't want to rid my dancer self from my bones. I wanted to reembody her. Writing would be how I could exhume that living dancer and finally be my real, full self.

DREAMS

Sometimes I feel very sad
(Can't find nothin' I can put my heart and soul into)

Brian Wilson
"I Just Wasn't Made for These Times" from *Pet Sounds*

Do you know what regret and loss sound like, what a vanishing dream sounds like for you? For me, they sound like "The Grand *Pas de Deux*" from the *Nutcracker Suite* by Peter Ilyich Tchaikovsky. Brendan (a trumpet player) loves to point out that it's just a play on a scale, but to me it is the strumming of my heart's strings.

Another musician mocked it by saying, "Tchaikovsky is SO melodramatic." Well, fine. But we dancers love a drama that can read all the way to the back of the house.

The weeping violins, swelling crescendos, moody decrescendos—I adore that music. I always have thought, though, that it's a bit much for the Sugar Plum Fairy. What does she have to be moody about? She's the ruler of Candyland, and there's not even a Lord Licorice. But in many versions of the ballet, choreographers have given the music to a Clara who becomes a grown-up ballerina in the second act. The drama makes sense from her perspective, because she's been through a lot! She defeated a mouse king, shrunk into some psychedelic fantasy, fell in love for the first time, and knows that it's all going to end. I always wanted to be Clara but never was given the part. In a way though, I feel like a real-life Clara. I fell in love, braved the obstacles, and enjoyed every fleeting moment of the dream before it evaporated around me.

All the feedback I heard and interpreted about God not wanting me to be a dancer made me skeptical from then on of any artistic urge or dream. I refused to allow myself to want anything big again. Suppression of ambition and desire became *modus operandi*. Before wanting to be a dancer, I had wanted to be a doctor. But did I do pre-med in college? No, I was too tired and depressed to do something difficult (and the pain level was still too intense to allow me to stand up long enough for a clinical rotation). I loved art history and quite nearly have a minor in it, but I didn't dare pour myself into something "frivolous" again. I decided that art was nonessential to life. I joined the University of Washington Business School for two reasons: earning potential (in case Brendan died young) and a desire to work in Human Resources and help people with their burdensome Labor & Industries cases. Except for lots of opportunities to "perform" as a well-spoken presenter and donor-favor-currier, Business School did nothing for my soul.

When I met people post-ballet, I knew they could not really become my friends or understand me unless they were told about my bad break-up with ballet. But I hated to tell it. My whole life as a dancer turned into a bad dream right at the end. In the Stowell/Sendak version of *Nutcracker* that I danced a hundred times, Clara is last seen terrified, confused, and weeping. That's how I felt too, and it's hardly a good state in which to make new friends or choose a new career path.

If people introduced me and said, "Jessica is a dancer," I imagined turning into the biggest Billy Goat Gruff and butting them in the stomach to send them right off the bridge. Instead, I made my body into a huge X while saying, "EX-dancer. EX."

I locked up the dancer part of me and not in some nice golden tower kind of way but in an abusive way, full of contempt. I stopped allowing myself to believe that art was important—to the world (like Mr. Hess always had taught me) or to me individually (which was a damn lie that I wished were true). I poured my perfectionism, my passion, and my work ethic into things that didn't bring me joy—things like a clean house, my GPA. The saddest part is that I decided I would probably never again feel true joy in my whole body and heart.

All the while, I was writing. Or drawing. The dancer-artist wanted out!

After Bran was born, a new dream to be a writer began to swell in my heart. It began as a little seed, but when my new understanding of God's never-ending flow of love began to water my soul, the seedling grew up so tall and so fast that I cowered before it. *No!* I thought. *Something bad will happen! What if I try and it doesn't work out? I'll never be able to try again.* Loving after loss is deeply challenging whether you had a miscarriage, a bad breakup, a rejection by the school or job you wanted, or a loss of your art or skill set. Trying to write with my hands while squinching my eyes shut and shrinking away like I might get hit is just too hard! Dreams themselves have a value that is worth mining. "Almost" does count.

All those days dancing on bloody toes, doing the difficult parts of being a dancer were only possible because the vision of what was to come carried me along. Bloody toes weren't the goal; Lincoln Center was. A contract with a ballet company, a life of moving and creating were what drew me through pain, loneliness, fear, and intimidation. If we cannot dream again, we have to push through on brute strength alone, and it just doesn't work. I quickly realized that without dreaming, without ambition, this writer thing could never happen.

I asked myself, "Why are you so scared to dream?" The answer seemed obvious: "Because I am afraid I'll be hurt again." And that's true, but I'm not a teenager. The writing world is not the ballet world (though it IS a good thing that I'm already very familiar with the words "Accepted" and "Rejected"). I'm not as vulnerable as I was because now I know I am loved no matter what. After some digging, I found my real answer.

"Why are you so scared to dream?"

"Because I have believed I was an idiot to dream the first time. It ended in nightmare, and I decided that was my fault. My bootstraps gave out. I wasn't tough enough to get the prize."

If someone else hurts me, I can choose to judge, protect myself for the future, and walk away. But if the enemy, the accuser, the shamer is me, how can I escape? I explained to myself that I earned, deserved the devastation that came to my ballet career and therefore to me. I couldn't possibly heal from the wound until I saw that there were two angles.

One: Someone made a mistake, and sadly I was injured in the accident. In this view, I was a victim, not a quitter or a weakling.

Two: I was a party to the tragedy, a train wreck that needed to be taught a painful lesson. In this second view, I am doomed to future pain and corrective measures coming in the form of tragedy unless I become perfect. Perfect is impossible; second best is putting my head down and never trying anything again.

Reality is that the accident was not my fault, but it changed my life by damaging my spine. Emotional turmoil was to be expected. However, my confused theology of suffering, aided and abetted by armchair philosophers and well-wishers, did a deeper more lasting kind of damage.

IN THE MIDDLE

And I won't get better
But someday I'll be free
'Cause I am not this body
That imprisons me

The Mountain Goats
"Isaiah 45:23" from *The Life of the World to Come*

For years, I have written honest, confused, heartfelt confessions and essays about dancing and my accident, but I have not ever provided the details, the play-by-play, like I've done for this book. I haven't wanted to look closely or let the memories, bad or good, back into my thinking brain. They hurt and make me angry, and it takes days to sweep them back into long-term storage. I end every piece of writing in a neat little bow. As soon as I let myself unspool, untangle, I cannot resist the urge to tie up all the ends, to make sense of it all.

* * *

For Christmas of 2017, Brendan gifted me some nights to write at my favorite hotel on Whidbey Island. After I wrote the chapter "Final Performance," I cried, sighed, and wandered my northwest modern hotel room throwing my hands in the air and pausing to stare out into the water as though something about the peace and vastness of the Saratoga Passage could gather me back up.

Questions I almost never ask forced their way from my gut to my mouth. "Why? Why did it have to be so hard? Why was it all so violent? Why did I have to be so alone?" You already know that at the time of the accident I gave myself answers to these questions before I even had time to finish saying them in my head. "It's God's will." That used to shut me up.

I pushed further that day on Whidbey Island.

Why? I don't know.

What does it mean that it was 'God's will?' I don't know.

Does that mean there is no room for grief? No.

No room for anger? No.

My need to think and pray about it all drove me down to the beach.

I've made it my practice on a Pacific Northwest shore to find "wishing rocks" as Brenna's family calls them. These are stones with a band of color running all the way around them in a connected circle. I'm not much for wishes, but I use them as opportunities to pray. I go out, open my heart to God, search, gather the rock in my palm, pray about something or someone, and throw the rock into the water like an offering.

Close to the lapping water, I asked God to meet me and started throwing rocks, each one a prayer asking why. My heart continued to be full of *I don't know! I don't know!* And then, *I don't know, but I hate it and wish none of it had ever happened!*

I stood straight and still, caught by my own surprising thought. That last bit wasn't true. Do I wish I could have danced longer and maintained my artistic community? Yes. Do I wish I'd not suffered so much physical and emotional pain? Yes. But am I sad over who I am right now? No. Not at all. I do not wish the accident had never happened. I love who I am. I'm not perfect; I don't love everything about me, but I love myself. I love the children that have come from my body. I love the friends I have. I love Brendan. I love everyone at Green Lake Presbyterian Church. I love God.

I am learning to be quiet and to listen for God to respond to me. Sometimes He does it with the sight of a rippling wave or a heron or eagle flying over me. Sometimes it's the power of the dark, low clouds driving above the water. Those things remind me that God is bigger and closer than I think. Never has he given me a palpable touch in absence of my family or friends. Always I hear him in song and bits of Scripture pacing through my mind.

The song that came as I walked along the beach beneath the Inn at Langley was not fancy, but it was my favorite hymn when I was a little girl. The song was "Trust and Obey," and here are the lines that repeated over and over in my mind:

When we walk with the Lord
in the light of his Word
What a glory he sheds on our way
While we do his good will
He abides with us still
And with all who would trust and obey

Maybe this is me trying to tie a bow, but I think it's a pretty one; and more importantly it is true. He *has* shed glory on my way. What a glory! He walked with me.

I might have been too hard on myself and truly suffered, but God was not unaware. Other people were too hard on me, and I was too hard on them. But God loves the offended and the offender. When I ran through the backstage passage after my fall, afraid and scolding myself, he was with me. Even that day of the PNBS "election" when I sat wishing for him to magically grab my hand, he spoke comfort to me through those lyrics stuck in my head, "the touch of his hand on mine." Even when I was four years old and left alone while my dad was in anaphylactic shock, God stayed with me. He kept the memory with me until I was old enough to see the sadness of it and finally comfort myself. And all through the moments I don't even remember, he was there.

* * *

On my way up the stairs back to my hotel room, another song's lyrics surfaced:

> *When through fiery trials thy pathway shall lie,*
> *My grace all sufficient shall be thy supply*
> *The flames shall not hurt thee*
> *I only design thy dross to consume*
> *and thy gold to refine*[1]

In my twenties, I took words like this to mean that God intentionally lays my path through fire, that he *designs* and *plans* to burn the sin out of me. How else could I ever be worthy of his approval? Throughout my life, approval had been the ultimate embrace I desired. But the God of the Bible does not say he will make us perfect and only then approve of the finished project.

We think of refinement as the process of making something pure. But perhaps we have too narrow a view of what "pure" means in the spiritual sense. As I trudged up from the beach, I heard the song's lines in a new, wider way. What if they just mean our pathways will pass through valleys of death's shadow, through fires, floods, loss, sadness, disappointment, and pain, but God provides grace for the terrible journey and may even shed glory on the way?

Scripture seems clear that everything works for the good of those called according to God's purpose. To me that means every circumstance can and will *result* in a child of God being somehow benefited. But I formerly understood those promises to mean that the main *goal* of all suffering was moral improvement. Now I know that's not enough. An understanding of his grace and perception of his glory must also be aspects of refinement.

Because God is perfect, result (what happens) is synonymous with goal (what he intended to happen). But maybe with human perspective we should separate result and goal. It is helpful to me, a finite, imperfect being, to trust that refinement will be a result of our fires but to never presume that trials have come solely for our improvement or our punishment. I particularly apply this perspective when encountering the trials in other people's lives. We have a few narrative examples in Scripture of suffering, humans, and God's stated opinion appearing in one place and time, like in the Book of Job, the story of Lazarus's resurrection, and the story of the man born blind. Each of them teach that God's glory and relationship with us are emphasized over the moral improvement or status of individuals.

I challenge the assertion that the "flames shall not hurt thee." They do hurt. When gold is refined, it is melted. The state of it is completely changed! Smelting hurts, but it does not destroy. We are never burned *up*, decimated altogether.

I think the reason I don't tend to ask the painful "Why" question is that a false presumption has muted the question. Here it is: "You don't need to ask 'Why.' You already know! Bad things happen so you'll be refined. Your only response should be, 'Thank you, sir. May I have another?'"

This smacks of a little ballet student being repeatedly abused by the teacher who "just wants you to be a good dancer." And doesn't the girl want to be a good dancer? Yes! More than anything! So she absorbs the abuse, tries to sift for the kernel of instruction or truth hidden somewhere in the abrasive, offensive delivery, and applies it. She is operating with the narrow view of purity: perfection only. But God does not want perfect automatons. He wants relationships with loving worshipers! God is not an abusive coach only willing to deliver teaching through pain and humiliation. He is a Father, a Lover, a Hero in pursuit of his beloved.

"Thank you, sir. May I have another?" is the reaction of a young woman faced with shocking, devastating pain. To know that disaster—natural, criminal, or otherwise—can come without cause or explanation and without any way to control it is absolutely horrifying. Unless she has or is developing a robust understanding of God's own grief over disaster, his grace for criminals and victims, and his commitment to making everything new again, she can never sit with grief and just let it be. Instead it *must* have use or explanation. But we can drive ourselves crazy looking for those answers.

I do believe that God uses every circumstance to accomplish his grand purposes, and that is a general comfort. But declaring or even guessing at the specific reasons God allows particular conditions and events in individual lives has the potential to bring further trauma or confusion to one another.

Can I explain genocide? Can I explain unjust imprisonments? Mass kidnappings and rape? Mental and physical illness in children? In anyone? Of course, I can't! I'm certain that a God strong enough to do anything about circumstances like these also may have ultimate reasons for allowing them to persist, but that doesn't mean I can know them or that God is pleased by them.

In my case, many voices, including my own, equated my accident with God's conduit for his refiner's fire. We assumed the intention and desired result was my moral improvement, but that is only one aspect of sanctification. I hope I have learned some humility, a gentleness for others, and greater gratitude because of my ballet loss. But moral improvement is a shallow prize compared to the height, width, and depth of the love of God! The cry of my heart for once-and-for-all approval is not satisfied by God slowly making me perfect. It is quieted by his LOVE. His closeness to me is the true prize. My sufferings have given me eyes and ears that see and hear him more clearly.

Psalm 40 is one of my favorites and a kind of artist's statement I adopted for myself. The writer reveals: *"In sacrifice and offering you have not delighted, but you have given me an open ear. Burnt offering and sin offering you have not required."* The notes in my English Standard Version Bible state that in Hebrew the words are "ears you have dug for me." The psalmist speaks of rescue from a miry pit. He begs God to protect him from those who want his harm. He admits he is threatened by evils from without and iniquities from within. But there in the center of his song, he tells God what he has learned about who God is. In my own words, he says:

> God, you don't want my rote performance. You don't expect moral perfection from me, but you have dug ears for me. Through my salvation and circumstances you have broken through my inability to hear who you truly are and what you are like!

Digging is hard work. God is passionate for relationship with us in spite of the hardness and darkness that aim to blunt his sharp advance.

> *I have told the glad news of deliverance in the great congregation:*
> *Behold, I have not restrained my lips, as you know, O Lord.*
> *I have not hidden your deliverance within my heart;*
> *I have spoken of your faithfulness and your salvation;*

I have not concealed your steadfast love and your faithfulness from the great congregation.
Psalm 40:9–10

* * *

While I consciously suffered through the accident and its aftermath, I didn't grasp its full depth or mourn sufficiently at the time. I was unable to acknowledge the injustice of the incident and the devastation of its effects As a young dancer, I had learned that my usefulness and value were in my compliance and endurance, not in my ability to stand up for myself or even in an ability to emote as my real self! My job was to make the company look good, to cover and excuse the bad things that happened—things like mental-health-destroying pressure, sexual harassment, insults, and careless stage accidents. With that kind of ingrained attitude, I looked at God, another powerful authority, as though he might be like them. But God does not need me to make him look good, to protect his power and his image by quickly and glibly explaining away the bad things that happen in his world. I have been made in God's image. If he can acknowledge the disgusting brokenness of the world, so can I.

God is a God of justice. He is not mad at me for getting hurt, but I bet he is mad that someone hurt me. God is perfectly capable of crying with me and being angry for me, of hating what happened to me AND saying to me, "Fear not. I am with you always" (Matthew 28:20). I could not absorb at the time the gravity and severity of the accident, so I skipped over grief right to the end, the moment of "See? It's all part of God's good story and plan for me."

But the story of the world is not done. We are in the middle where it gets bad, where the plot thickens, where the characters hurt each other and make giant mistakes, where people look up from car accidents and stage accidents and ask "Why?!"

I'm certain, as a person of faith, that the end will be good. Words like heal, restore, repair, renew, rebuild, and reclaim fill my vision of eternity. But this is just the middle, and while we may know that "it all turns out OK in the end," we don't know the resolution of every character's individual plotline. When we watch someone die—whether literally or figuratively—on our way to the "everything is great now" end, we can still cry and wish *that* moment didn't have to go *that* way. "Why did they have to kill her off?" we say. "She was so great!"

The only answer is, "I don't know. We'll have to wait and see. It's not over yet."

LOSING MR. HESS

April 2016

I should have wrote a letter
And grieve what I happen to grieve

Sufjan Stevens
"Should Have Known Better" from *Carrie & Lowell*

I think about him all the time. Through his teaching, he is in my thoughts every day. He is in the way that I live.

But now Mr. Hess is dead. I will never visit and introduce him to my four children: a storyteller, a musician, an artist, and a dancer. He would have found them delightful. I will never sit with him for a cup of tea and excitedly tell him all the stories from my time in the professional ballet life that proved him right. I won't ever be able to thank him for telling me the truth, for forming my goals and dreams in my heart, and for behaving like I could achieve them. I can't cry to him about the parts that hurt. I can't ask him to remind me about why art is so important, why I should love being an artist and continue to chase. I will never write the letter explaining why I didn't talk to him for his final fifteen years.

When I read on Facebook that he had passed away, the wave of shock kept me quiet for hours and hours. By the next day, I was ready to examine my regret. I let myself lose touch with him because of shame. I considered myself a failure as a dancer and artist, and so I never went to him any more when I went home in the few months he was still there. Then he and Mrs. Hess left Amarillo, and I never wrote. I could not imagine writing tear-stained letters about what really happened to me.

I was afraid he would think I gave up too easily, and even I knew better than to torture myself imagining what Mrs. Hess might say. I was too young to know these fears were best left alone. Shame was the last thing I ever needed to feel around Mr. Hess. I never went to him for comfort, just approval. I couldn't see past dancing as the only way to earn his smile. The only vision I ever had of pleasing him showed me onstage or maybe teaching ballet. I would have liked to have a richer relationship than just student-pleasing-teacher. We had enough affection for one another to support real give-and-take. I had been working up the nerve to write a letter that could begin an adult friendship, but I was too late.

I thought there was still time. When someone is in the very fabric of your life, you forget that he is just a human. He was like some kind of Gandalf to me, or a tree in the woods you consult for wisdom, an icon of the theater, a legend that would always be. Surely, someone like that would never die. I always pictured him still thinking and making art. I imagined I would get ready and begin my relationship with him again as an adult.

Oh, I miss him badly.

The good news is that he used his life to teach and show, so

I have his work with me forever. If he could have the influence and power for good that he had, then I can too. He wasn't the magical character I saw him as when I was young. He was a man who loved art and people, and through the pursuit of his passions he made a profound impact on the world. What if he looked at how everything ended badly in Amarillo after decades of work there and felt ashamed, wondered about the value of his career there? I would have rushed to tell him how important he was and shown him reciprocal love and encouragement. To me and hundreds of others, he was a treasure. He is the reason I know it's wrong to ignore art.

* * *

I love you, Mr. Hess.

I'm sorry I did not write. I will miss you always, but I remember what you said. You said if I worked hard and kept trying, good things would happen. You were right. A lot of good things have happened.

I do wonder why you never alerted me that this could all end in failure. Sometimes I wish you had. You might have told me what to do if I almost became a dancer. You spoke so eloquently and often about the successes that I assumed you were disappointed with the unsuccessful and therefore wouldn't speak of them. Maybe you would have explained what you made of mistakes and losses if I had asked you. Looking back, I'm sure you would have, but I think my own sense of pride left me determined to never need to ask about or report any failure. If we had talked about it, then maybe you could have shifted my perspective. When things "didn't work out," I might not have been so ashamed. I cannot know.

I never did quit though. I never quit working hard, not for one second. You would have seen that. I put myself through college. I got a job. I kept trying to go back and take ballet class even though it hurt. I stayed (and stay) with the man I love. I sunk to the bottom of the pit of despair and dug through the slimy, wet mud until I eventually found treasure there. I was given ears to hear God. I strained to look up and see light, to feel strong hands moving me to climb.

If I had a company full of dancers, I would watch them survive an impossible *adagio*, see them double over to breathe, notice their hands rubbing tired hamstrings. I'd stop the music and slowly turn to look into the middle-distance above their heads.

"People," I'd say and take my lipstick out of my pocket.

"People, you must remember." The lipstick would go on a bit crooked because I'd be unwilling to stop talking long enough to get it right.

"You must remember that if you work hard and keep trying, good things will happen." I would smile as I pictured you.

"But bad things will happen too." The room would get very still.

"It never ends in failure, though. Not if you can remind yourself that you have no idea when the end is. We are in the middle, and until the day you die, anything can happen in the middle. An artist's life must be one of constant metamorphosis. If dancing doesn't work out, for heaven's sake be a dancer doing something else. When you almost become something, that only means there is room for more."

Re-rolling my sleeves, of course I'd add, "Now do it again. And straighten your knees."

* * *

I don't have a room full of dancers. But Mr. Hess, I know there is more work to be done, more art to be found and made.

HAPPY NEW YEAR

Old teenage hopes are alive at your door
Left you with nothing but they want some more
Oh, you're changing your heart
Oh, you know who you are

Feist
"1, 2, 3, 4" from *The Reminder*

Two round chocolate cakes are cooling on my kitchen counter. Let it be known: they are box mix cakes. But the ganache will be homemade. Tomorrow is my New Year's Day, my birthday, and this birthday means I am one-half Texan and one-half Seattleite (and the Seattle grows stronger everyday). I feel them, the two halves.

Tonight is New Year's Eve, and I am doing what other people do on December 31st. I'm taking stock, choosing words, evaluating the last 364 days and 33 years, dreaming dreams, making plans. Ever since I stood at Magnuson Park with the birds and decided to begin looking for what happened to the dancer inside me, I have experienced contractions of my soul as someone new gets ready to show up. I didn't know the pains were labor or growth. I just felt a discomfort, a disquiet.

The other day at the zoo in the python habitat, the sleek, enormous snake lay resting behind its old skin. I think of him hurting, itching, moving to leave what once worked for him in order to be a little bigger.

Rather than behaving like one who is loved and free, I have been a slave to expectations for thirty-three years. I've just wanted desperately to make everyone happy and get whatever kind of hug is available. But tonight I feel like a snake able to stretch to a new length. I feel as though a tight membrane of restriction around my heart—some alien pericardium—finally ruptured, and now my soul can breathe and expand more fully. I recall the popping sensation of my water breaking when I labored for Bran. It was a relief and a reassurance that the baby really was coming. The spiritual version is more satisfying even than that, and I'm so excited to try to be the woman who is being (re)born.

I am a dancer.

I find joy, delight, and clarity in performance, practice, and pursuit of perfection. I want to learn new steps. I want to allow myself to be bad at them, but still love how they feel and how they look, so much so that I will flop about like an idiot until I nail it. The steps are no longer French verbs, but things like gardening, writing a song, writing my first fiction, playing a plastic ukulele I bought on Amazon, and drawing my family members over and over again. I care a lot about creating perfect cocktails and meatballs. I want to party, and listen, and watch people. I want to be able to mimic exactly everything I love about the people around me just like I wanted to move my head like Suzanne Farrell or straighten my knees like Gelsey Kirkland. I want to be silly and carefree backstage even as I know how to keep it professional and work hard the rest of the time. I still want to be Elise, someone reliably kind and funny.

I get it now. I'm an EX-dancing body, but I will always be a dancer. Now I just have to trust that I'll never, ever get thrown out. The only director I really have is God, and he will never drive me away. I don't have to keep my injuries, my weaknesses, and my insecurities secret. There is no understudy waiting for me to fail.

God has given me permission to be the exact person he made me to be. I need not fear that doing the things that I think are beautiful, good, and fruitful are inherently selfish, wrong, or dangerous. I don't have to look at every difficulty in my life like it signifies God's immense disappointment in me. Being able to say "I am a dancer" is great, but the best thing is that I'm not *just* a dancer. I am one whole person and can be free of the desperation to please people. A person willing to almost have something will always have more than those who can only accept absolute success.

Will there be things I have to give up? Surely. Absolutely. I have certainly learned that these last seventeen years. Will there be things that seem right and good to me but *are* selfish, wrong, or dangerous? Probably. And I may have to discover that the hard way sometimes. I will suffer again. People will hurt me, and I'll hurt them. But I trust God to stay with me as he has my whole life. My every effort to make art, to change, to love others must flow from my knowledge of his presence with me.

Other people may not always get it. They might judge how I spend my time or energy, but I don't answer, ultimately, to people. Sometimes God wants different things from me than people do. Who am I worried will disapprove, or shame, or scold me? Both everyone and no one in particular. The judges, juries, and executioners mostly exist in my mind. They are an amalgamation of all the fears of rejection I've ever felt and every judgment I have passed. But I am not rejected. I am deeply loved by God.

CHAPTER ONE

Hope deferred makes the heart sick,
But a desire fulfilled is a tree of life.

Proverbs 13:12

"Ed is looking for you," Emily said as I greeted her in the sanctuary door Sunday morning.

"Oh. OK!" Naturally, I thought I was in trouble. One doesn't shake fear of judgment and rejection in a day.

I saw Ed approaching. "Hey, you need me?" I asked.

"Oh, yeah! There is a girl here who is seventeen and just moved here to dance at the Pacific Northwest Ballet, and I thought, 'Wow, you need to meet Jessica.'"

I spun around to pick her out of the congregants, a task I knew would be easy. It felt like Christmas. I tripped over people, pushing to get to this girl.

I launched right into my introduction: "Hi! I just heard you are here to go to PNB! I was a PD for a few years and then worked in the school for a while after that."

"Oh, cool!" she said. Then I convinced her to go to a church picnic with Brendan, the kids, and me.

Now I love her. She is all the things I imagine were present in me the first time I walked into Green Lake Presbyterian Church. Certainly, she possesses much that I don't. For one thing, she has perfectly long, straight, New York City Ballet hair. She is her own complicated, fresh young woman, and I look forward to getting to know who she really is. But Sunday morning, I strained to see her as anything but a ghost of myself.

* * *

A few years earlier, there were another couple ballerinas, sisters, who came through the church. But my heart was not ready to receive them. I wanted to know and help them in any way I could, but it hurt. I didn't know how to be honest with them. How could I say, "I'm still dying inside over what I lost. I'll never be the same, and I hope you will be protected from the terrible fate I met in that place" without seeming like a total freak. People-pleasing, young dancers are in no way prepared to deal with brokenness. At least, I wasn't when I was in their position. Back then I would have seen the modern day, truth-telling, emotional me as a crazy person, a negative person (one may say "weird"). I would have responded kindly, maybe even with wisdom, but the judgments I made internally would have been harsh. Young me would have presumed that older me did something to screw up. When I met those first few ballet girls, I hadn't yet given myself permission to still be a dancer, so I felt like a loser. Loving people even while being a reject is Jesus-level stuff. It was beyond me.

The new PD's first Sunday at Green Lake was seventeen years and one week after mine. As a fellow, experienced dancer, I felt a magnetism for her. I wanted to love her, not because I should, but because I do. We've barely begun to get to know each other, but I know she loves ballet. I know she is brave, polite, flexible, dedicated, and self-possessed. She is one of those people who can do what I did, and so without consuming a pound of salt together, I already know she is a kindred spirit. I'd bend over backwards for her. She deserves love and support, peace and reassurance.

Maybe someday she'll have to text me to say she has been injured (I hope not, but it is possible). I will weep and drive her to physical therapy. I'll get on the phone and listen to her mother cry too. I'll buy her favorite flowers, order Thai food for her, and try to keep the spiritual Band-Aids in the bottom of my purse where they belong. Maybe she'll be promoted to the company, and I'll weep and laugh. I'll take her out to a fancy dinner and let her drink my champagne. I'll attend every performance. I'll clap and whoop! No matter what, I'll pray for her and ask that she always know that she is a dancer

just like I am.

EPILOGUE

To get ready to write, I have to stop noticing all the reasons I shouldn't do it. I look away from the dishes, assure myself that leftovers are a fine meal, and refuse to put a new load of laundry in the machine. If there is no babysitter, I shoo kids into the backyard or set them up next to me with scissors, paper, and crayons. If I have a babysitter, I peel my two-year-old off my neck, smile, kiss him, and give him to her.

As I slide my laptop into the beautiful, hand-quilted case sewn for me by a friend, I manage emotions: excitement, fear, insecurity. I say to myself, *This is NOT a waste of time. The only way to fail is to not try at all.* I also think, *At least no one is going to push me off the scenery.* And, *There's no understudy. Only I can write this story, so if I don't, it will be gone.*

On my way to the coffee shop, I decide which document to open, which chapter to change, or which new story to tell. I scope out a good table, one with space for my laptop, a plate, and a drink. I stake my claim before I even order, especially if a table by the window opens up. I need the window for staring and wondering.

I speak warmly to the barista while I wait for her to fill my teacup with Vanilla Jasmine, and then I take the hot mug to my table. I open the laptop, plug in my headphones, and choose music to accompany me. I go to my Google Drive, take a deep breath, and click open my draft.

Inevitably, a tiny ballet student from the studio up the block will come in for a snack with her grown-up. We smile at one another, and I say, "I hope you enjoy your dancing today."

NOTES

The Ballet Class

1. Cathy Marie Buchanan, The Painted Girls (New York City: Riverhead Books, 2013), 43.

In the Middle

1. John Rippon, "How Firm a Foundation, Ye Saints of the Lord." 1787.

ACKNOWLEDGMENTS

Thank you to my parents for loving me and understanding the value of ballet in my life (and teaching me to write!).

Thank you, Whitney, for being my sister.

Thank you to Doug Serven and White Blackbird Books for supporting this book.

Thank you to the best neighbors on earth, Roy and Kalin.

Thank you to Wedgwood Javasti, Third Place Pub, and Elliot Bay Brewing Lake City in Seattle. Also Prima Bistro, Useless Bay Coffee Company, and Inn at Langley on Whidbey Island. You provided studios for me as I learned how to dance on the page.

To Mr. and Mrs. Hess's children and grandchildren: I have written passionately here about your mother and father. I loved them deeply, and I'm grateful for the ways you shared them throughout your lives. You inspired me because of how they spoke about you, so their pride and love for you can only have been profound.

Lone Star Ballet of the nineties: You are my dance family forever, and I miss you everyday.

Trinity Church Seattle, past and present, we are one body,

so I need you and love you very much. To Michael Kelly, Anna Van Wechel, and David Richmon in particular: your teaching and personal counsel represent the parental advice and support of God in my life.

To Kay Klein: it occurs to me that you are the Mr. Hess (but better) of my midlife. Your consistent, wise, protective, insightful counsel has been a key in God's hands to unlock me. And I so wanted to be opened up again.

To the Pacific Northwest Ballet of 2019: Thank you for your performances and contributions to the art. I love you and my season tickets.

To Mr. Halby, Ellen Hope, Caroline Fleming, Jodi Rea, Wendy Casper, and Denise Bolstad: I loved working with you. In such a challenging post-traumatic setting, the only explanation for all the fun and joyful memories I have is you.

My fellow Professional Division students, especially Kari, Carla, Stayce, Drew, Anne, Randi, Kiyon, David, Josh, Laura, Lucien, Lauren, George, and Sean: I adore you. What would I have done without you? Your value is immeasurable.

To the Riberas: Dan, Laura, Mark, Katie, Jordan, and Candiece: Thank you for the love, enthusiasm, support, and babysitting!

To Edward Nudelman, genius: Thank you for being patient, kind, and honest in your editing and hand-holding. I needed a teacher, and you were excellent.

Dearest beloved friends: How can I ever thank you enough? Brenna, Blythe, Bethany, Blaze, Becky, Karen, Libby, Elisabeth, Elizabeth, and Amanda, your support, reading, frantic text answers, tear-wiping, inspirational pep talks, and examples are jewels in your eternal crowns. I love you! And, Blaze, this cover and your generosity astound me.

To my children, Ezra, Ivo, Hazel Belle, and Bran: If I accomplish anything with this book at your expense, shame on me. You deserve my best, my deepest love, and my energy. You are so, so cool and inspire me. Thank you for your cheerleading!

Finally, Brendan: I'm not sure I even understand how immense a blessing you are in my life. Thank you for never once behaving like this was trivial or stupid (massive fears). You received the most hideous tears and behaviors I've ever offered, and you love me anyway. I cannot believe I have you.

ABOUT THE AUTHOR

Jessica Ribera writes creative nonfiction in Seattle. Her work has appeared in *Fathom Magazine, Scary Mommy, Brevity Nonfiction Blog, Feminine Collective, The Mighty,* and *Co-laborers, Co-heirs: A Family Conversation.*

She is married to Brendan. They have four children together.

You can follow her at https://thealmostdancer.com.

ABOUT WHITE BLACKBIRD BOOKS

White blackbirds are extremely rare, but they are real. They are blackbirds that have turned white over the years as their feathers have come in and out over and over again. They are a redemptive picture of something you would never expect to see but that has slowly come into existence over time.

There is plenty of hurt and brokenness in the world. There is the hopelessness that comes in the midst of lost jobs, lost health, lost homes, lost marriages, lost children, lost parents, lost dreams, loss.

But there also are many white blackbirds. There are healed marriages, children who come home, friends who are reconciled. There are hurts healed, children fostered and adopted, communities restored. Some would call these events entirely natural, but really they are unexpected miracles.

The books in this series are not commentaries, nor are they meant to be the final word. Rather, they are a collage of biblical truth applied to current times and places. The authors share their poverty and trust the Lord to use their words to strengthen and encourage his people. Consider these books as entries into the discussion.

May this series help you in your quest to know Christ as he is found in the Gospel through the Scriptures. May you look for and even expect the rare white blackbirds of God's redemption through Christ in your midst. May you be thankful when you look down and see your feathers have turned. May you also rejoice when you see that others have been unexpectedly transformed by Jesus.

Made in the USA
Coppell, TX
07 December 2019